Also by Francine Segan

SHAKESPEARE'S KITCHEN

# MOVIE MENUS

VILLARD Ⓥ NEW YORK

# MOVIE MENUS

Recipes for Perfect Meals with Your Favorite Films

## FRANCINE SEGAN

A Villard Books Trade Paperback Original

Copyright © 2004 by Francine Segan

All rights reserved under International and Pan-American Copyright Conventions. Published in the United States by Villard Books, an imprint of The Random House Publishing Group, a division of Random House, Inc., New York, and simultaneously in Canada by Random House of Canada Limited, Toronto.

VILLARD and "V" CIRCLED Design are registered trademarks of Random House, Inc.

Library of Congress Cataloging-in-Publication Data
Segan, Francine.
   Movie menus: recipes for perfect meals with your favorite films / Francine Segan.
      p.   cm.
   Includes bibliographical references and index.
   ISBN 0-8129-6992-8 (trade pbk.)
      I.  Title.
   TX652.S44 2004
   641.5—dc22   2003055574

Printed in the United States of America on acid-free paper

Villard Books website address: www.villard.com

98765432

BOOK DESIGN BY CASEY HAMPTON

TO MARC, WHO ALWAYS SHARES HIS POPCORN

# ACKNOWLEDGMENTS

Have you seen the movie *Awakenings*? It's based on a book by Oliver Sacks, who also wrote *The Man Who Mistook His Wife for a Hat*. Well, around our house, my husband is called the Man Who Mistook an Oyster for a Mushroom.

In the early stages of working on my first book, *Shakespeare's Kitchen*, I asked my husband, Marc, to taste-test a variety of savory Elizabethan pies I was developing. When he claimed to like the mushroom one best, I knew that my beloved, accomplished in so many areas, had nonetheless a Neanderthal palate. Not one of the pies was a mushroom pie. Not one of them had even a hint of mushroom. No truffles, no truffle oil, nothing that had anything remotely to do with mushrooms. What he had actually liked best was the oyster pie. (Incidentally, none of the other taste-testers liked it, so oyster pie never made it into the book!)

From then on, I have "depended on the kindness of strangers," enlisting friends, relatives, students, doormen, the wonderful staff at my all-time favorite bookstore—Kitchen Arts and Letters, in New York City—and, well, anyone who'd stand still long enough for me to pop something into his mouth. I'd like to acknowledge my gratitude to all those brave palates.

A big thank-you also to the outstanding professionals at Random House for all their assistance, especially Todd Doughty, Laura Ford, Casey Hampton, Beth Pearson, Stacy Rockwood, and Krista Vossen.

And lastly, my deepest thanks go to chef and food stylist Wes Martin for his help in developing many of the recipes, and to my talented, enthusiastic editor, Mary Bahr. To quote George M. Cohan, "My mother thanks you, my father thanks you, my sister thanks you, and I thank you."

# CONTENTS

## CHAPTER 4—AMERICA'S EARLY YEARS

## CHAPTER 5—THE WILD WEST

## CHAPTER 6—THE GILDED AGE

## CHAPTER 7—THE WAR YEARS

## CHAPTER 8—GANGSTERS TO GREASERS

## CHAPTER 9—ROMANTIC DINNER FOR TWO

## CHAPTER 10—FAMILY MOVIE NIGHT

# INTRODUCTION

**M**ovie Menus celebrates the foods and dining customs of the past, inspired by our favorite movies, with recipes from authentic historic cookbooks, re-created and modernized for contemporary tastes.

If you have ever wondered what Russell Crowe might really have eaten if he were a gladiator, or imagined what Gwyneth Paltrow would have dined on with Shakespeare, or asked yourself just what would have been sizzling on John Wayne's campfire at the Alamo, this is the book for you.

Besides tempting recipes from the past, Movie Menus is seasoned with interesting film and culinary trivia throughout every chapter. Movie Menus will answer movie and food lovers' questions such as:

Which was the only sequel ever to win a Best Picture Oscar? What was cherries jubilee originally created to celebrate? What hit movie was the first completely computer-generated full-length feature? Which is the highest-grossing Western of all time? What was a cowboy's favorite put-down for lousy grub? Which star of a classic war film refused his Academy Award? What did the real Marc Antony do to impress Cleopatra? How did Kirk Douglas persuade other stars to join the cast of Spartacus? What movie has the line "I'll have what she's having"? What was the first food to be rationed during World War II?

Divided into ten chapters, each featuring a different film genre, *Movie Menus* includes recipes for and trivia on historic epics, Westerns, war stories, gangster flicks, romantic comedies, and family films. Each chapter also contains a how-to section on giving a themed movie party and a detailed list of suggested films in each genre.

So, if you like good movies and great food, whether you want to host an Oscar party or just want to serve something different for dinner, you'll find *Movie Menus* as fun to read as it is to use.

# MOVIE MENUS

# PHARAOHS AND PHILOSOPHERS: ANCIENT TIMES

**COMING ATTRACTIONS**

MILK AND HONEY GRIDDLE BREAD ★ HERBED OLIVE PUREE

CHICKPEA DIP ★ MINTY GARLIC SPREAD ★ ASSORTED STUFFED FIGS

**FEATURE PRESENTATION**

LAMB ON SKEWERS WITH MINT MARMALADE ★ CHICKEN FROM ANCIENT AFRICA

SHRIMP WITH FETA ★ PEA AND DILL PUREE

**CLOSING CREDITS**

STUFFED DATES ★ PEACHES IN SPICED WINE

**LIGHTS, CAMERA, ACTION! FINGER-FOOD BUFFET**

MOVIE SUGGESTIONS

Hollywood epics inspired by the Bible and ancient Egypt, Greece, and Rome include some of the best films ever created. Pyramids, mummies, gladiators, Roman conquerors, and the Greek myths make for exciting adventures. Who can forget scenes like the parting of the Red Sea in *The Ten Commandments,* the chariot race in *Ben-Hur,* and Russell Crowe's battles in *Gladiator?*

These spectacular movies help bring the past to life, and sampling a meal of that time can further enhance the experience. This chapter explores the foods and dining customs during that vibrant age and serves up a tasty menu created from ancient writings and archaeological finds. Many recipes come from the Roman *On Cookery,* thought to be the oldest surviving cookbook. Other recipes are taken from *The Philosopher's Banquet,* written by a Greek living in ancient Rome, detailing the foods and dining customs of Greece's golden age.

The ancients dined reclining on couches, and although they ate some admittedly strange things, like stuffed mice, roasted flamingo tongue, and grilled cow womb, they also enjoyed familiar favorites such as pizza, focaccia, and lasagna. There are many interesting taste combinations to rediscover from their time.

So, sit back—or rather, lie back—and dine like a Roman emperor while you watch your favorite epic and try some of these succulent dishes, which can be served meze-style, on shared platters, eaten with fingers, as was done in antiquity.

# MILK AND HONEY GRIDDLE BREAD

SERVES 6

☆  ☆  ☆

In *The Ten Commandments,* Charlton Heston's real-life infant son played the baby Moses.

This recipe for moist and flavorful griddle bread is a reminder of the flatbreads that the Jews, led by Moses, ate during their exodus from Egypt. Delicious alone or wrapped around salami or grilled asparagus, it's also great for scooping up stews and dips.

4 OUNCES FETA CHEESE

3 TABLESPOONS HONEY

½ TEASPOON SALT

½ CUP ALL-PURPOSE FLOUR, PLUS MORE AS NEEDED

OLIVE OR VEGETABLE OIL

1.  In a large bowl, mash the feta, honey, and salt together with a fork until well combined. Add the flour and mix until a dough forms. Using your hands, knead the dough in the bowl until smooth. Cover in plastic wrap and allow to rest, at room temperature, for about 20 minutes.

2.  Divide the dough into 12 equal portions and on a very lightly floured work surface roll each section into a very thin circle, about 3 inches in diameter.

3.  Lightly oil a nonstick pan and over medium-low heat cook the circles until golden, about 1 minute per side. Serve warm.

---

*And I felt His words take the sword from my hand!* —CHARLTON HESTON, *BEN-HUR*, 1959

*Ben-Hur* was the first film ever nominated for twelve Academy Awards and ties for the record of most won, eleven, with *Titanic. Ben-Hur* earned actor Charlton Heston his only career Oscar.

Theaters did not sell food during the showing of *Ben-Hur,* as the movie was considered too important to allow for the usual popcorn chomping.

# HERBED OLIVE PUREE

SERVES 10

*Somebody put too many olives in my martini last night.*

W. C. FIELDS, *NEVER GIVE A SUCKER AN EVEN BREAK*, 1941

☆  ☆  ☆

Olives, which according to Greek myth are a gift from the goddess Athena, were an important part of the ancients' diet. They were eaten with bread and crushed to make oil, which was considered good for the body both inside and out. This dip, a recipe from the Roman statesman Cato, is not only perfect with pita bread or toasted baguette slices but also delicious tossed with cooked spaghetti.

It's one of my favorite recipes because it can be made days in advance and only gets better with time, just like a good movie.

½ CUP PITTED WHOLE OIL-CURED BLACK OLIVES

½ CUP PITTED WHOLE BRINE-CURED GREEN
    OLIVES

¼ CUP CHOPPED ONION

¼ CUP EXTRA-VIRGIN OLIVE OIL

1 GARLIC CLOVE, MINCED

1 TEASPOON FENNEL SEED

1 TEASPOON GROUND CUMIN

1 TEASPOON GROUND CORIANDER

¼ CUP MINCED FRESH PARSLEY, MINT, AND BASIL

GRATED ZEST OF 1 LEMON

6 PITA BREADS, CUT INTO QUARTERS AND
    WARMED

1. Combine the olives, onion, olive oil, garlic, fennel seed, cumin, and coriander in a food processor and puree until smooth. Place in a small bowl, cover with plastic wrap, and allow the flavors to mingle at room temperature for at least 6 hours.

2. Stir well and top with the minced herbs and lemon zest. Serve with the warm pita bread sections.

---

*Arrange food, drink, entertainment, and a sit-down orgy for forty.*

—LEON GREENE, *A FUNNY THING HAPPENED ON THE WAY TO THE FORUM*, 1966

Ancient Greek feasts were an all-male event; and sexual relations between men, an accepted norm.

While it may have been accepted in 200 B.C., Hollywood censors certainly didn't accept it in A.D. 1960. The seduction scene between Laurence Olivier and Tony Curtis was cut from the original *Spartacus* and only added back in the 1991 restoration. Since the sound track had been lost and Sir Laurence was dead, Anthony Hopkins dubbed his dialogue.

# CHICKPEA DIP

SERVES 10

*Truly, this man was the son of God.*

JOHN WAYNE, *THE GREATEST STORY EVER TOLD*, 1965

☆　☆　☆

This quote is John Wayne's only line in the movie *The Greatest Story Ever Told.* According to Hollywood legend, the Duke kept delivering the line stiffly, so after several failed readings the director pleaded with him to try it once more "with awe." On the next take, Wayne supposedly said, "Aw, truly this man was the son of God."

Chickpeas, eaten for centuries, make a deliciously creamy and healthy dip for veggies or corn chips. Once you try this, you'll never go back to store-bought. Truly.

| | |
|---|---|
| 1 LARGE ONION, DICED | 1½ CUPS VEGETABLE OR CHICKEN STOCK |
| ½ CUP OLIVE OIL | SALT AND PEPPER |
| 1 CUP DRIED CHICKPEAS, SOAKED OVERNIGHT, RINSED, AND DRAINED | 2 LARGE GARLIC CLOVES, CHOPPED |
| | JUICE AND GRATED ZEST OF 1 LEMON |
| 1 TEASPOON DRIED OREGANO | MINCED FRESH MINT |
| 1 BAY LEAF | PITA BREAD QUARTERS OR CORN CHIPS |

1. Sauté the onion in ¼ cup of the olive oil in a large saucepan over medium heat until golden, about 10 minutes. Add the chickpeas, oregano, bay leaf, and stock. Bring to a boil. Reduce the heat and simmer until the chickpeas are tender and the stock is absorbed, about 1 hour. Discard the bay leaf, season to taste with salt and pepper, and allow to cool slightly.

2. Put the mixture into a food processor along with the garlic, lemon juice, and remaining ¼ cup olive oil. Pulse until well combined but still coarse.

3. Serve the chickpea dip topped with the lemon zest and mint and accompanied by pita quarters or corn chips.

---

*Who loves ya, baby?* —TELLY SAVALAS, *KOJAK* (TV SERIES), 1973

Telly Savalas first shaved his head to play Pontius Pilate in *The Greatest Story Ever Told.* He liked it so much that he kept it that way for the rest of his career.

# MINTY GARLIC SPREAD

SERVES 10

*There are never enough hours in the days of a queen, and her nights have too many.*

ELIZABETH TAYLOR, *CLEOPATRA*, 1963

☆　☆　☆

The sexual exploits of Cleopatra, who had children with both Julius Caesar and Marc Antony, were legendary. So too were the exploits of Elizabeth Taylor, who although married to Eddie Fisher during the filming of *Cleopatra* nevertheless carried on a very public affair with costar Richard Burton.

This wonderfully tangy mint-and-garlic spread comes from an ancient Roman cookbook and is great with raw or grilled veggies. Perfect for your next affair.

3 CUPS CUBED ITALIAN BREAD, CRUSTS ON

3 TABLESPOONS FRUIT VINEGAR

4 GARLIC CLOVES, MINCED

2 TABLESPOONS HONEY

½ TEASPOON GROUND CORIANDER

½ TEASPOON GROUND CUMIN

½ CUP GRATED PARMESAN CHEESE

½ CUP EXTRA-VIRGIN OLIVE OIL

SALT AND PEPPER

⅓ CUP FRESH MINT LEAVES

ASSORTED RAW OR GRILLED VEGETABLES AND FLATBREADS FOR DIPPING

1.　Place the bread cubes in a food processor. Mix the vinegar into ½ cup water, pour over the bread, and toss. Let stand until the bread is soft and has absorbed all the liquid, about 10 minutes.

2.　Add the garlic, honey, coriander, cumin, and Parmesan. Puree until smooth. Slowly add the olive oil and continue to puree until incorporated. Season to taste with salt and pepper. Add the mint leaves and pulse a few times to incorporate. Serve in a bowl surrounded by assorted vegetables and flatbreads.

---

*—Milk? For beasts of prey?*

*—They are only great cats, wife, do you not hear them purr?*

—PUPELLA MAGGIO AND JOHN HUSTON, *THE BIBLE*, 1966

In the movie *The Bible,* Noah fills his ark with tame and wild animals of all sorts, including cats. Hollywood, it seems, likes cats, as there are a slew of films starring felines, including my family's favorites: *The Adventures of Milo and Otis; The Aristocats; The Big Cat; The Cat from Outer Space; Harry and Tonto; Homeward Bound: The Incredible Journey; Oliver and Company; That Darn Cat;* and *The Three Lives of Thomasina.*

# ASSORTED STUFFED FIGS

SERVES 6

*He's got to have a weakness! Because, you know, everybody has a weakness.*
*For Pandora, it was the box thing. For the Trojans, hey, they bet on the wrong horse.*

VOICE OF JAMES WOODS, *HERCULES,* 1997

☆   ☆   ☆

Greek athletes, including the legendary Hercules, had a weakness for figs and ate them as a regular part of their strength-building diet. The role of Hercules has been played in films by real-life strongmen Arnold Schwarzenegger and Steve Reeves.

Dried figs, plumped in wine and then filled with either prosciutto, mascarpone, or pistachios, make for an irresistible appetizer that doesn't require herculean efforts to prepare.

18 DRIED FIGS

1 CUP WHITE WINE

1 TABLESPOON MASCARPONE CHEESE

GRATED ZEST OF ½ LEMON

2 TABLESPOONS FINELY CHOPPED PISTACHIO NUTS

1 TEASPOON HONEY

2 OUNCES THINLY SLICED PROSCIUTTO, CUT INTO TWELVE ½-INCH-WIDE STRIPS

1. In a small saucepan, bring the figs and wine to a simmer and cook until the figs are soft, about 5 minutes. Remove the figs and continue cooking the wine until very thick and syrupy, about 10 minutes. Reserve.

2. Cut about ¼ inch off the tops of 6 figs and set the figs upright on a serving platter. Top each with ½ teaspoon of the mascarpone and sprinkle with the lemon zest.

3. Remove the stems from 6 more figs and halve the figs lengthwise. Put the pistachios on a plate and dip each fig half into the chopped nuts. Drizzle with the honey. Arrange on the serving platter.

4. Remove the stems from the remaining 6 figs and halve the figs crosswise. Make a small indentation in each fig center with the tip of your finger or edge of a knife. Roll a strip of the prosciutto into a bundle and stuff into each fig half. Drizzle about ½ teaspoon of the wine syrup over each fig half and add them to the serving platter.

To play a sleep-deprived character in *Marathon Man,* Method actor Dustin Hoffman went three days without rest. When his costar Laurence Olivier saw Hoffman's ragged state, he quipped, "Dear boy, you look absolutely awful. Why don't you try acting? It's so much easier."

The marathon got its start in ancient Greece, where, according to legend, a soldier ran 24.8 miles from the town of Marathon to Athens to announce Greece's victory over Carthage. The Olympics, too, originated in ancient Greece, where beginning in 776 B.C., the games were held in the town of Olympia to honor the god Zeus. The very first modern Olympic Games were held in Athens in 1896.

# LAMB ON SKEWERS WITH MINT MARMALADE

SERVES 8

*Have you noticed the nastiest of tyrants are invariably thin?*

CHARLES LAUGHTON, *SPARTACUS*, 1960

☆   ☆   ☆

Ancient Romans did not use forks. Instead, eating only with the right hand, they delicately picked up morsels with their fingers. This finger-licking marmalade is also great with beef or chicken.

| | |
|---|---|
| ¼ CUP FRUIT VINEGAR | 1 CUP FRESH MINT LEAVES |
| 2 TABLESPOONS RAISINS | 3 TABLESPOONS OLIVE OIL |
| 4 DATES, PITTED AND MINCED | SIXTEEN 1-INCH CUBES OF LAMB |
| 1 TEASPOON HONEY | (ABOUT 1 POUND) |
| 2 TABLESPOONS PINE NUTS | SALT AND PEPPER |
| 2 TABLESPOONS GRATED PARMESAN CHEESE | 8 SMALL WOODEN SKEWERS, SOAKED IN WATER |

1. Put the vinegar, raisins, dates, and honey in a small saucepan and simmer over medium heat until the raisins are soft, about 3 minutes. Allow to cool to room temperature.

2. Put this mixture, along with the pine nuts and Parmesan, in a food processor and puree until smooth. Add the mint leaves and pulse until minced. Slowly add the olive oil and continue blending until smooth.

3. Toss the lamb cubes with half of the mint marmalade. Cover with plastic wrap and refrigerate for at least 1 hour and up to 12 hours. Season the remaining marmalade with salt and pepper to taste. Cover and refrigerate.

4. Preheat the broiler or a grill pan.

5. Liberally season the lamb cubes with salt and pepper. Place two lamb cubes on each wooden skewer and broil or grill until the lamb reaches the desired doneness, about 1 minute per side for medium.

6. Serve with the reserved marmalade on the side.

> *What is more stupid than this, a man building a ship on dry land?*
>
> —ONLOOKER, *THE BIBLE*, 1966
>
> In the movie *The Bible,* director John Huston cast himself as Noah after he was unable to get Charlie Chaplin for the part. Even though *The Bible* was the highest-grossing film that year, it did not earn an Oscar nomination in any category.

# CHICKEN FROM ANCIENT AFRICA

SERVES 6

*Shall we agree, you and I, upon what Rome really wants, has always wanted of Egypt—*
*corn, grain, treasure. It's the old story. Rome was built upon Egyptian riches.*

ELIZABETH TAYLOR, *CLEOPATRA*, 1963

☆   ☆   ☆

This Roman recipe was originally named for Numidia, a country in ancient Africa. Numidia, like Egypt, supplied Rome with food, marble, and wild animals for amphitheater events.

Serve this aromatic and delicious sweet-spicy stew with large spoons and plenty of rice to savor every drop.

⅓ CUP ALL-PURPOSE FLOUR

1 TEASPOON GROUND CORIANDER

1 TEASPOON COARSELY GROUND PEPPER

½ TEASPOON GROUND CLOVES

½ TEASPOON GROUND CINNAMON

½ TEASPOON GROUND ALLSPICE

½ TEASPOON GROUND CUMIN

4 BONELESS, SKINLESS CHICKEN BREASTS
    (ABOUT 6 OUNCES EACH), CUBED

SALT

¼ CUP PEANUT OIL

2½ CUPS CHICKEN STOCK

¼ CUP WHITE WINE VINEGAR

½ CUP CHOPPED PITTED DATES

1 TABLESPOON HONEY

1 TEASPOON WORCESTERSHIRE SAUCE

1 TEASPOON BOTTLED HORSERADISH

4 OUNCES ARUGULA OR MUSTARD OR
    DANDELION GREENS, CHOPPED

2 TABLESPOONS CHOPPED FRESH CILANTRO

1.  Preheat the oven to 375 degrees.

2.  Mix the flour, coriander, pepper, cloves, cinnamon, allspice, and cumin in a large bowl. Season the chicken generously with salt and dredge it in the seasoned flour until well coated. Save any excess flour.

3.  In a large Dutch oven, heat the peanut oil over medium-high heat. Add the chicken cubes and brown on all sides, about 4 minutes per side. Transfer the chicken to a plate. Add the stock and vinegar to the pan and bring to a boil, scraping up any bits clinging to the pan. Stir in the leftover flour along with the dates, honey, Worcestershire sauce, and horseradish. Add the chicken, cover, and bake for about 30 minutes, or until the sauce is thick and bubbly.

4.  Remove from the oven, mix in the arugula and cilantro, and serve.

# SHRIMP WITH FETA

SERVES 4

*"Trust," the word has always made me apprehensive. Like wine, whenever I've tried it the aftereffects have not been good. I've given up wine and trusting.*

REX HARRISON, *CLEOPATRA*, 1963

☆　☆　☆

Marc Antony wanted to impress Cleopatra with his fishing skills, so he secretly positioned swimmers under their barge to attach fish to his line. At some point, the slaves ran out of live fish and attached dried instead!

The feta and herb topping takes only minutes to assemble, and adds an impressive flavor to shrimp or your favorite fish.

¼ CUP DRIED BREAD CRUMBS

3 OUNCES FETA CHEESE, CRUMBLED

1 TABLESPOON OLIVE OIL, PLUS MORE AS NEEDED

1 TABLESPOON DRIED DILL

1 TABLESPOON DRIED CHIVES

SALT AND PEPPER

1 POUND MEDIUM SHRIMP, PEELED AND DEVEINED

1. Preheat the oven to 400 degrees.

2. Combine the bread crumbs, feta, olive oil, dill, and chives in a small bowl. Generously salt and pepper the shrimp and put them on a lightly greased baking pan. Top with the bread crumb mixture. Bake, uncovered, for about 10 minutes, or until the shrimp are firm and cooked through.

---

*Everything that deceives may be said to enchant.* —PLATO, 428–348 B.C.

Plato's words could apply to Hollywood, where cinematic deceptions certainly enchant us. The Romans, too, enjoyed deceptions. To amuse guests, Roman chefs served whimsical dishes, often with one ingredient disguised as another. For example, liver pâté was served in a fish mold and called "fish without fish."

In true Roman—and Hollywood—fashion, Kirk Douglas, who coproduced *Spartacus*, practiced a little deception of his own. To attract as many big-name stars as possible, he showed each actor a different script, with his or her character's part beefed up.

# PEA AND DILL PUREE

SERVES 8

☆　☆　☆

This delicious Roman side dish was originally named after Commodus, son of the emperor Marcus Aurelius. In the movie *Gladiator,* Commodus was depicted as an evil villain who killed his own father, declared himself emperor, and fought as a gladiator. The real Commodus did not kill his father but did perform as a gladiator. At the time, it was considered very eccentric behavior for an emperor and was just one of the many reasons Commodus was eventually assassinated.

1 LARGE PURPLE ONION

2 TABLESPOONS OLIVE OIL

ONE 10-OUNCE PACKAGE FROZEN BABY PEAS, THAWED

$\frac{1}{3}$ CUP WHITE WINE

$\frac{1}{3}$ CUP CHOPPED FRESH DILL

SALT AND PEPPER

1. Sauté the onion in the olive oil in a skillet over medium heat until golden, about 10 minutes. Add the peas and wine, raise the heat to high, and boil until the wine is almost completely absorbed, about 5 minutes.

2. Puree the warm pea mixture with the dill in a food processor or blender. Season to taste with salt and pepper. Serve warm.

---

*I will win the crowd. I will show them something they've never seen before.* —RUSSELL CROWE, *GLADIATOR*, 2000

*Gladiator,* which won five Academy Awards, is about a general who becomes a slave. Forced to battle as a gladiator, his only hope of freedom is in impressing the spectators. In ancient Rome, slaves, prisoners, and even captured enemy soldiers were often compelled to perform as gladiators. Only very rarely did free men, attracted by the potential for riches and fame, voluntarily join.

# STUFFED DATES

*Gladiators don't make friends. If we're ever matched
in the arena together, I have to kill you.*

WOODY STRODE, *SPARTACUS*, 1960

☆   ☆   ☆

Gladiators trained hard, eating dried fruits like dates and figs to build stamina and muscle. A collection of gladiator statistics that included the fighter's favorite weapon and number of victories was found under the ashes in the ruins of a private home in Pompeii. The ancients, it seems, collected gladiator stats then the way we collect baseball cards today.

Simple to prepare, these stuffed dates offer the delicious combination of sweet and spicy so popular in antiquity.

12 SMALL DATES

3 TABLESPOONS COARSELY CHOPPED ALMONDS

1 TABLESPOON COARSELY CHOPPED WALNUTS

½ CUP RED WINE

2 TABLESPOONS HONEY

¼ TEASPOON PEPPER

6 OUNCES SEMIHARD CHEESE, SUCH AS
CHEDDAR OR THE GREEK CHEESE
KEFALOGRAVIERA, CUT INTO WEDGES

1.  With a sharp knife, make a small cut lengthwise through the top of each date and remove the pit.

2.  In a small dry nonstick pan, lightly toast the almonds and walnuts over medium-low heat.

3.  Using a teaspoon, fill the dates with the nut mixture.

4.  In a small saucepan, combine the wine, honey, and pepper and simmer over medium heat for about 15 minutes. Place the dates in the pan and continue to simmer until they are warm, about 5 minutes.

5.  Serve the warm dates with the cheese wedges.

---

*At my signal, unleash hell.* —RUSSELL CROWE, *GLADIATOR*, 2000

Russell Crowe, who won an Oscar for Best Actor for *Gladiator,* broke his foot, gashed his cheek, and fractured his hip during the filming.

Crowe's character, Maximus, was shown fighting in Rome's 50,000-seat Colosseum, which got that name some time after the eighth century. In gladiator days, it was called the Amphitheatrum Flavium.

---

# PEACHES IN SPICED WINE

SERVES 4

*—My father is rolling over in his grave.*

*—Your father is alive.*

*—This will kill him.*

JACK GILFORD AND ZERO MOSTEL, *A FUNNY THING HAPPENED ON THE WAY TO THE FORUM*, 1966

☆　☆　☆

Chocolate, vanilla, and coffee, all favorite dessert flavors, were unheard of in ancient Greece and Rome. Those New World ingredients were not introduced into Europe until after the time of Columbus.

You'll love these luscious cumin-flavored peaches, a refreshing change from the usual after-dinner sweets.

3 PEACHES, PEELED AND THINLY SLICED

2 TABLESPOONS HONEY

1 CUP DESSERT WINE

1 TEASPOON GROUND CUMIN

Divide the peach slices among 4 large wineglasses and top them with the honey. Pour ¼ cup of the wine into each glass and sprinkle with the cumin. Serve immediately.

# FINGER-FOOD BUFFET

The ancient Romans ate while lying down on couches. Not so different from us modern-day couch potatoes! For my toga finger-food buffet, I push the furniture to the side of the room and spread couch cushions and large pillows out on the floor. Not only does that let a large group of friends sit comfortably around the video screen, but it also more authentically re-creates how they really ate in antiquity. I also like to scatter flower petals on the floor, as was done then, and to set out wooden bowls filled with whole fruit, nuts, and bay leaves for added color and scent.

For atmosphere, I drag in a few terra-cotta planters and some stone lawn sculptures (or rather, I enlist my son and husband to do the dragging). I top the buffet table with draped white sheets because white, the color of fine marble, reminds me of ancient Greece and Rome. Candles, clusters of ivy, and crockery jugs add drama. Our toga parties are usually informal family affairs, cooked up on Saturday mornings. When the fancy hits, we telephone four or five other families and invite them to come for dinner and an epic. In antiquity, of course, invitations were extended in person at the public baths, or delivered by messenger. If you decide to mail invitations, you might like to write them on roughly torn cooking parchment paper or on postcards of Greek and Roman ruins.

In antiquity, wine was more potent than it is today, so it was often served sweetened and diluted with water or ice. Inspired by how the ancients drank, I like to serve Spartacus Spritzers. Mix half a glass of inexpensive red wine with a teaspoon of honey and top with a splash of seltzer, for a light refreshing toast to the past.

## Movie Suggestions

### THE BIBLE

*The Bible,* 1966. The first twenty-two books of Genesis, starring Richard Harris, John Huston, and George C. Scott.

*David and Bathsheba,* 1951. Lush biblical tale starring Gregory Peck and Susan Hayward.

*The Greatest Story Ever Told,* 1965. Story of Christ's life, starring Charlton Heston.

*Jesus Christ Superstar,* 1973. Movie based on the smash-hit rock musical.

*Samson and Delilah,* 1949. Victor Mature and Hedy Lamarr star in the biblical story of Delilah, who robbed Samson of his strength.

*The Ten Commandments,* 1956. Story of Moses. DeMille's last movie, a remake of his 1923 silent film, stars Charlton Heston and Yul Brynner.

### ANCIENT EGYPT

*Cleopatra,* 1963. Epic about Egypt's queen, starring Elizabeth Taylor, Richard Burton, and Rex Harrison.

*Land of the Pharaohs,* 1955. Story of the building of the pyramids, starring Joan Collins and Jack Hawkins.

*The Mummy,* 1932. Classic mummy horror tale starring Boris Karloff.

*The Mummy Returns,* 2001. Archaeologists uncover mummies and trouble.

*The Mummy's Tomb,* 1942. Lon Chaney Jr. stars.

*Prince of Egypt,* 1998. DreamWorks animated film about Moses, with voices of Val Kilmer, Michelle Pfeiffer, and Steve Martin.

*The Scorpion King,* 2002. Archaeologists uncover more trouble; stars the Rock.

## ANCIENT GREECE

*Alexander the Great,* 1956. Richard Burton plays the fourth-century-B.C. Greek conqueror.

*Atlantis: The Lost Empire,* 2001. Disney animated film.

*Helen of Troy,* 1956. Tale of Zeus's daughter Helen, whose love for the Trojan prince Paris caused a war.

*Hercules,* 1997. Disney animated film.

*Iphigenia,* 1977. In Greek with English subtitles. Tragedy by Euripides about King Agamemnon's plans to sacrifice his daughter to the gods.

*Jason and the Argonauts,* 1963. Crowd-pleasing adventure about the quest for the Golden Fleece.

*The Trojan Horse,* 1962. Stars Steve Reeves and John Barrymore.

*The Trojan Women,* 1971. Starring powerhouse actresses Katharine Hepburn and Vanessa Redgrave.

## ANCIENT ROME

*Battle of the Valiant,* 1963. Barbarians invade Rome.

*Ben-Hur,* 1959. Jew battles Roman imperialists; famed chariot race; record eleven Oscars. Must see.

*Caesar and Cleopatra,* 1945. Based on George Bernard Shaw's play. Stars Claude Rains and Vivien Leigh.

*Caligula,* 1980. Very R-rated story of ancient Rome, with John Gielgud and Peter O'Toole.

*Demetrius and the Gladiators,* 1954. Sequel to *The Robe.* Holy slave, bearing robe, is enlisted as one of Caligula's gladiators. Stars Anne Bancroft.

*The Fall of the Roman Empire,* 1964. Emperor Marcus Aurelius murdered by son Commodus. Stars Sophia Loren and Alec Guinness.

*A Funny Thing Happened on the Way to the Forum,* 1966. Musical starring Zero Mostel and Buster Keaton.

*Gladiator,* 2000. Stars Russell Crowe, whose performance as a general-turned-gladiator won him the Best Actor Oscar.

*Julius Caesar,* 1953. Shakespeare's play, starring actors Marlon Brando and John Gielgud.

*The Last Days of Pompeii,* 1960. Remake of 1935 film. Stars Steve Reeves.

*Quo Vadis?,* 1951. Story of Rome's emperor Nero, starring Robert Taylor and Peter Ustinov.

*The Robe,* 1953. Marcellus, played by Richard Burton, wins the robe of the recently crucified Christ in a dice game.

*Roman Scandals,* 1933. Lucille Ball makes her film debut in this comedy about a man who dreams himself back to ancient Rome.

*Spartacus,* 1960. Gladiator leads a rebellion against Roman oppression. Stars Kirk Douglas and Peter Ustinov. A must-see classic.

*Titus,* 1999. Shakespeare's lesser-known play, starring Anthony Hopkins and Jessica Lange. Be sure to eat *before* you see it!

# KNIGHTS AND KINGS: THE MIDDLE AGES

**COMING ATTRACTIONS**

INDIVIDUAL MEAT PIES ★ GOLDEN "APPLES" ★ ROAST GARLIC–SAFFRON TOASTS

**FEATURE PRESENTATION**

PENNE WITH SAFFRON CREAM SAUCE ★ NEAPOLITAN EGGPLANT

MEDIEVAL FRENCH "LARKS"

**CLOSING CREDITS**

SWEET CHERRIED CHEESE ★ DRIED FRUIT PUDDING

PEARS IN BERRY-WINE SYRUP

**LIGHTS, CAMERA, ACTION! MEDIEVAL FEAST**

MOVIE SUGGESTIONS

Fire-breathing dragons, wizards, fair maidens, chivalrous knights, King Arthur, Robin Hood, the Crusades—medieval times provide wonderful inspiration for moviemakers, and there are hundreds of films ranging from historical epics to comedies and fantasies about this spellbinding era. *The Lord of the Rings, The Adventures of Robin Hood, Dragonheart,* and *The Flame and the Arrow* are just a few favorites.

The dining customs and foods of the Middle Ages are a fascinating topic, and a medieval feast is a wonderful way to bring the period's pageantry and spectacle to your home.

The following recipes were inspired by actual surviving medieval cookbooks and will give you a taste of the kinds of foods eaten then. The recipes come from historically significant works, including *Le Viandier,* written circa 1375 by the French chef Taillevent, and *The Forme of Cury,* the first English cookbook, prepared for King Richard the Lion-Hearted in 1390. *The Forme of Cury* contains 196 recipes, including ones for gold-gilded pies, roast rabbit, pheasant, fish jellies, and spiced wines. Although Middle English is a little tricky to read, I've included a few of the original recipes from *The Forme of Cury,* or *The Method of Cooking,* as it would be called in modern English, to give you a feel for how they were written. I've also included a translated recipe from a medieval Italian cookbook.

Feasts then included whole boar, elaborate salads, tall multilayered meat pies, and one of my favorites, roasted peacock with its feathers back on, which seems to breathe fire thanks to the chef's trick of filling the beak with flammable cotton and igniting it just before serving.

Now, while I'm intrigued by the roast peacock recipe, I've certainly never tried it and you won't find it in this cookbook. There are no recipes for roast swan or "heads of beasts" either, even though they were typical feasting fare, too, but I have included a range of dishes that highlight the interesting taste combinations, beautiful garnishes, and whimsical medieval presentations popular then.

# INDIVIDUAL MEAT PIES

SERVES 10

*How dear of you to let me out of jail.*

KATHARINE HEPBURN, *THE LION IN WINTER*, 1968

☆　☆　☆

During the Middle Ages, "four and twenty blackbirds" really were baked in a pie! Or rather, they were placed live in an already baked, but hollow, piecrust. Unsuspecting guests cut into the pie, releasing the birds.

The combination of sweet dried fruits with meat and aromatic spices makes for just as irresistible a first-course dish now as in 1390.

8 OUNCES GROUND PORK OR BEEF

2 TABLESPOONS CURRANTS

2 TABLESPOONS PINE NUTS

6 DATES, PITTED AND FINELY CHOPPED

3 PRUNES, PITTED AND FINELY CHOPPED

1/4 TEASPOON GROUND NUTMEG

2 TABLESPOONS LIGHT BROWN SUGAR

2 TABLESPOONS ORANGE LIQUEUR OR ORANGE JUICE

1/2 TEASPOON SALT

1/4 TEASPOON PEPPER

ONE 17-OUNCE BOX FROZEN PUFF PASTRY, THAWED

1 LARGE EGG, BEATEN

1. Place the meat, currants, pine nuts, dates, prunes, nutmeg, brown sugar, liqueur, salt, and pepper in a bowl and mix well. Refrigerate for at least 1 hour, so the flavors can mingle.

2. Preheat the oven to 350 degrees.

3. Roll out the puff pastry 1/8 inch thick on a floured work surface. Using a 2 1/2-inch round cookie cutter, press out about 30 dough circles. Place 1 tablespoon of the meat mixture on each circle, fold in half, and pinch the edges to seal. Brush the top with the egg and place on a dry nonstick baking sheet. Bake for 20 minutes, or until golden brown.

ORIGINAL RECIPE: TARTLETES—Take veel ysode and grinde it smale. Take harde eyren isode and yground, & do therto with prunes hoole, dates icorue, pynes and raisouns coraunce, hoole spices & powdour, sugur & salt; and make a litell coffyn and do this fars therinne. Cover it & bake it & serve it forth. —*THE FORME OF CURY*, 1390

*That's not a knife.* That's *a knife.*

—PAUL HOGAN, *CROCODILE DUNDEE*, 1986

It was customary in the Middle Ages to arrive at a feast with your own knife, as even wealthy nobles seldom owned enough cutlery for everyone.

I was impressed to learn that in *The Lord of the Rings,* Viggo Mortensen performed all his own stunts, insisting on battling with actual steel swords instead of the lighter aluminum or rubber ones usually used in filming.

# GOLDEN "APPLES"

SERVES 8

*Merlin, make me a hawk!*
RICHARD HARRIS, *CAMELOT*, 1967

☆  ☆  ☆

Medieval chefs delighted diners with special effects. Edible sculptures of meat, marzipan, or dough were made into everything from coats of arms to animals, fruits, flowers, and even the likenesses of special guests.

These saffron-flavored meatballs, with sage-leaf stems, look like tiny golden apples. A grape tucked in the center of each, as directed in the original instructions, not only helps the meatball keep its shape but provides a refreshing taste surprise.

| | |
|---|---|
| 8 OUNCES GROUND VEAL OR PORK | ¼ TEASPOON GROUND NUTMEG |
| ¼ CUP DRIED WHOLE WHEAT BREAD CRUMBS | ¼ TEASPOON GROUND CLOVES |
| 1 LARGE EGG | PINCH OF SAFFRON THREADS |
| 1 TABLESPOON DRIED THYME | 16 SMALL GREEN SEEDLESS GRAPES |
| 2 TABLESPOONS DRIED PARSLEY | 16 FRESH SAGE OR PARSLEY LEAVES, WITH |
| ½ TEASPOON SALT | STEMS |

1. Preheat the broiler.

2. Combine the meat, bread crumbs, egg, thyme, parsley, salt, nutmeg, cloves, and saffron in a bowl. Divide the mixture into 16 equal portions. Wrap each portion around a grape and form an apple shape.

3. Place the meatball apples upright on a well-greased pan, and broil 4 to 5 inches from the flame for 4 minutes, or until cooked through. Using a toothpick, gently insert a sage leaf into the top of each. Serve warm.

---

*—Why, you speak treason!*
*—Fluently.*
—OLIVIA DE HAVILLAND AND ERROL FLYNN, *THE ADVENTURES OF ROBIN HOOD*, 1938

Burt Lancaster did all his own swashbuckling, high-flying stunts for *The Flame and the Arrow*. Lancaster's longtime acrobatics partner, Nick Cravat, played his sidekick, Piccolo. Cravat just couldn't seem to lose his Brooklyn accent, though, so his character had to be rewritten as a mute.

# ROAST GARLIC–SAFFRON TOASTS

SERVES 6

*A Wizard is never late, Frodo Baggins. Nor is he early.*

*He arrives precisely when he means to.*

IAN MCKELLEN, *THE LORD OF THE RINGS: THE FELLOWSHIP OF THE RING*, 2001

☆ ☆ ☆

This recipe from a fourteenth-century medieval Italian cookbook was originally made as a pie. However, in this modern version, the filling, which is made with garlic that has become very sweet and mild after roasting, is spread on toasted baguette slices for an easy-to-prepare treat for whenever guests arrive.

| | |
|---|---|
| 4 WHOLE HEADS GARLIC | PINCH OF GROUND NUTMEG |
| OLIVE OIL | SALT AND PEPPER |
| ½ CUP HEAVY CREAM | TOASTED BAGUETTE SLICES |
| PINCH OF SAFFRON THREADS | 2 BACON STRIPS, COOKED AND CRUMBLED |
| 4 OUNCES GOAT OR FETA CHEESE | |

1. Preheat the oven to 400 degrees.

2. Coat the garlic heads with a little olive oil and place them on a roasting pan. Bake for 50 minutes, or until the garlic is soft.

3. Meanwhile, simmer the cream and saffron in a small saucepan over medium heat until reduced by half, about 10 minutes.

4. Once cool, remove the garlic cloves from their skins and put them into a food processor with the reduced cream, goat cheese, and nutmeg. Blend until smooth. Season to taste with salt and pepper.

5. Serve the spread on toasted baguette slices, topped with the crumbled bacon.

---

*Cancel the kitchen scraps for lepers and orphans, no more merciful beheadings, and call off Christmas!*

—ALAN RICKMAN, *ROBIN HOOD: PRINCE OF THIEVES*, 1991

In the Middle Ages, instead of plates, food was eaten from large dried slices of bread, which were often colored and flavored with herbs and spices. "Trenchers," as they were called, were changed between courses and given to the poor who waited outside the noblemen's gates for leftovers.

# PENNE WITH SAFFRON CREAM SAUCE

SERVES 6

*We're the sons of peasants. Glory, and riches, and stars are beyond our grasps.*
*But a full stomach, that dream can come true.*

ALAN TUDYK, *A KNIGHT'S TALE*, 2001

☆　　☆　　☆

Ravioli and macaroni are medieval Italian inventions, at the time so labor-intensive and expensive that only the rich could afford them. Macaroni such as penne was made in those days by rolling dough around a stick and drying it in the sun. Making pasta dough and ravioli is still time-consuming, so in this modern version of a ravioli recipe from the Middle Ages, I prepare the yummy filling ingredients as small meat patties and serve the patties in a golden medieval saffron sauce with store-bought pasta. The taste is just as spectacular, but with a fraction of the effort.

| | |
|---|---|
| 2 CUPS HEAVY CREAM | 1 TEASPOON SUGAR |
| PINCH OF SAFFRON THREADS | 1/2 TEASPOON GROUND GINGER |
| 1 SLICE WHITE SANDWICH BREAD, CRUST | PINCH OF GROUND CLOVES |
|    REMOVED | SALT AND PEPPER |
| 8 OUNCES GROUND CHICKEN | 1 TABLESPOON OLIVE OIL |
| 8 OUNCES GROUND PORK | 1 LARGE ONION, THINLY SLICED |
| 1/4 CUP PLUS 1 TABLESPOON GRATED PARMESAN | 1 POUND PENNE PASTA |
|    CHEESE | 1/4 CUP CHICKEN STOCK |
| 1/2 CUP WHOLE MILK RICOTTA CHEESE | PINCH OF GROUND TURMERIC (OPTIONAL) |
| 1 LARGE EGG | 2 TABLESPOONS CHOPPED FRESH PARSLEY |
| 1 TABLESPOON DRIED PARSLEY | |

1. Put the cream and saffron into a deep saucepan and bring to a low boil over medium heat. Lower the heat to maintain a gentle simmer and cook until reduced by half, about 15 minutes.

2. Meanwhile, in a large bowl, mash the bread with a few tablespoons of warm water until pulplike. Add the chicken, pork, 1/4 cup Parmesan, ricotta, egg, parsley, sugar, ginger, cloves, and salt and pepper to taste and mix until well combined. Form a heaping tablespoon of the meat mixture into a small patty about 1/4 inch thick. Repeat with the remaining mixture. You should have about 24 patties. In a large nonstick skillet, heat the olive oil over medium-high heat. Cook the meat patties, turning once, until golden and cooked through, about 1 minute per side. Transfer to a plate; cover to keep warm.

3. Meanwhile, bring a large pot of water to a boil and salt it generously. Add the onion and penne, stir, and cook according to package directions, until the pasta is al dente. Drain and place the pasta and onion in a large serving bowl.

4. Stir the chicken stock and 1 tablespoon Parmesan into the hot reduced cream. Season to taste with salt and pepper. The sauce should be a golden color due to the saffron. If you would like a more intense color, add the pinch of turmeric. Add the meat patties, including any liquid they released while resting. Pour the saffron cream sauce and meat patties over the penne and onion and toss until evenly coated. Top with the parsley and serve immediately.

---

*It's all for nothing if you don't have freedom.* —MEL GIBSON, *BRAVEHEART*, 1995

Today's stars are free agents, able to accept or refuse movie projects at will. Mel Gibson, for example, had the clout and freedom to produce, direct, and star in *Braveheart*, the 1995 movie about a thirteenth-century Scotsman who battles English oppression.

During the so-called golden era of Hollywood from the twenties to the forties, stars were seldom so free. Bound by ironclad contracts, actors were subject to the whims of powerful studios. Olivia de Havilland was so outraged by the terms of her contract that in 1941 she sued the studios, claiming that their self-extending clause violated the Thirteenth Amendment of the Constitution and was equivalent to slavery. She won but for several years after was offered fewer film roles.

# NEAPOLITAN EGGPLANT

SERVES 6

*If I could ask God one thing, it would be to stop the moon.*
*Stop the moon and make this night and your beauty last forever.*

HEATH LEDGER, *A KNIGHT'S TALE*, 2001

☆   ☆   ☆

Clocks, rare and expensive during the Middle Ages, were certainly not something you'd ever find in a lowly kitchen. Medieval cooks had to rely on different measures such as the look and feel of food to know when a dish was done. In this original recipe, for example, the charming directions advised that the eggplant be cooked for no longer than it takes to say "two Our Father's."

This sweet-and-sour eggplant side dish, which also makes a great appetizer, is an ancestor to the modern Italian caponata, only much, much faster and easier to make. This must-try recipe is one of my favorites.

2 LARGE EGGPLANTS

SALT

3 TABLESPOONS OLIVE OIL

½ CUP SHERRY VINEGAR

2 TABLESPOONS DARK BROWN SUGAR

3 GARLIC CLOVES, MINCED

PEPPER

CHOPPED PITTED BRINE-CURED GREEN OLIVES AND DRAINED CAPERS (OPTIONAL)

1. Preheat the oven to 500 degrees.

2. Peel and dice the eggplants into 1-inch cubes. Lightly salt the cubes and allow them to drain in a colander for 15 minutes to reduce any bitterness.

3. Gently dry the eggplant on a paper towel, pressing out any excess moisture. Coat a roasting pan with the olive oil and add the eggplant cubes. Gently stir the cubes so they are coated in the oil and spread them out into one layer. Bake, stirring occasionally, for about 25 minutes, or until golden.

4. Meanwhile, in a small bowl, mix the sherry vinegar and brown sugar together until the sugar is dissolved, and then add the garlic.

5. Transfer the cooked eggplant from the roasting pan to a serving platter. Add the vinegar mixture to the roasting pan and stir to scrape up any bits in the pan. Return the pan to the oven and bake for about 3 minutes to soften the garlic. Remove the pan from the oven and pour the liquid over the eggplant. Stir well to combine and season to taste with salt and pepper. Top with the olives and capers, if using.

6. Serve as a side dish or on toasted baguette slices as an appetizer.

ORIGINAL RECIPE: EGGPLANTS—Get eggplants and wash and peel them well, then set a little water on the fire and bring them to a boil; cut them into quarters and add a little salt to the water; do no let them boil more than two Our Father's; then take them out onto a cutting board and let them drain; coat them in flour and fry them; when they have fried, drain off almost all of the oil; get a clove of garlic, grind it up with a quarter-piece of the eggplants; then get a little oregano, of the sort that is put on anchovies, grind it up with the garlic and a little bread, pepper, saffron and salt; then distemper all of this together with verjuice and a little vinegar and throw everything together into the pan to fry a little; then dish it out and serve it with mild spices.

—*CUOCO NAPOLETANO*, FIFTEENTH CENTURY

*Geoffrey Chaucer's the name, writing's the game.* —PAUL BETTANY, *A KNIGHT'S TALE*, 2001

It's hard to believe, but they had etiquette books back in Chaucer's day. One medieval book on manners instructed diners not to lick greasy fingers or wipe them on their clothes but advised using the tablecloth instead.

# MEDIEVAL FRENCH "LARKS"

SERVES 6

*I merely chewed in self-defense, but I never swallowed.*

VOICE OF SEAN CONNERY, *DRAGONHEART*, 1996

☆  ☆  ☆

Peacocks, although regularly served at feasts, were considered tough and tasteless birds. Smaller birds like larks, although not as spectacular, were preferred for flavor.

This recipe, by a fourteenth-century French chef, was originally for lark stuffed with cheese and roasted with pancetta and bay leaves. In this modern version, I substitute thinly sliced beef for the lark but keep the other tasty ingredients.

6 THIN SLICES TOP ROUND (ABOUT 1 POUND)

6 SLICES PROSCIUTTO

½ CUP SHREDDED CACCIOCAVALLO OR
    MOZZARELLA CHEESE

2 TABLESPOONS DRIED BREAD CRUMBS

1 TABLESPOON CHOPPED FRESH PARSLEY

¼ TEASPOON PEPPER

¼ LARGE ONION, LAYERS SEPARATED

6 BAY LEAVES

1. Preheat the broiler.

2. On a work surface, lay the beef slices flat and top each with a slice of prosciutto. In a small bowl, stir together the cacciocavallo, bread crumbs, parsley, and pepper. Divide the filling among the meat slices and spread it evenly over the prosciutto. Starting with the narrow end, tightly roll the meat into bundles.

3. Cut the onion layers into 12 segments about 1 inch wide and 2 inches long. Put 6 of the onion segments on a greased baking sheet and lay a bay leaf in the cradle of each segment. Lay a meat bundle, seam side down, on the bay leaf in an onion segment. Repeat with the remaining bundles and top each with another onion segment.

4. Broil for about 4 minutes per side, or until the onion and meat begin to brown. Remove the "larks" from the oven and transfer to a serving platter. Serve immediately.

> *I'll have what she's having.*
>
> —ESTELLE REINER, *WHEN HARRY MET SALLY*, 1989
>
> Not everyone at a medieval feast ate the same food. Special dishes such as roast peacock and swan were served only to the guests of honor. It was also just the more important guests who were seated near the then-expensive salt, which is where we get the expression "below the salt." Another expression, "the upper crust," also dates from the Middles Ages and comes from the fact that the best slices from the top of the bread were only offered to the guests of honor.

# SWEET CHERRIED CHEESE

SERVES 6

*The pellet with the poison's in the vessel with the pestle;*
*the chalice from the palace has the brew that is true.*
DANNY KAYE, *THE COURT JESTER*, 1956

☆   ☆   ☆

Clinking our glasses together is a custom from the Middle Ages. According to legend, knights would bang their cups together to combine the liquids and assure each other that neither was poisoning the other. The expression "drink a toast" started in the Middle Ages, too, where pieces of toasted bread were added to beer and wine for flavor.

Serve this delicious no-bake dessert in wineglasses for a perfect toast to the past.

15 OUNCES WHOLE MILK RICOTTA CHEESE
¼ CUP CONFECTIONERS' SUGAR
2 OUNCES FRUIT LIQUEUR, SUCH AS KIRSCH OR CHAMBORD
DASH OF ROSE WATER (OPTIONAL)
⅓ CUP FRESH PITTED CHERRIES OR FROZEN PITTED CHERRIES, THAWED
GRATED ZEST OF 1 LEMON

1. Mix the ricotta, confectioners' sugar, liqueur, and rose water, if using, in a blender until smooth, about 3 minutes. Add the cherries and pulse until just incorporated. Place in a bowl, cover with plastic wrap, and refrigerate for at least 1 hour before serving.

2. Serve in wineglasses, topped with the lemon zest.

---

*When there are no more dragons to slay, how will you make a living, knight?*
—VOICE OF SEAN CONNERY, *DRAGONHEART*, 1996

Phil Tippett, who won the Visual Effects Oscar for his creations in *Jurassic Park,* also designed Draco, the forty-three-foot-long fire-breather in *Dragonheart.*

# DRIED FRUIT PUDDING

SERVES 6

*Wrong or right, they have the might, so wrong or right,*
*they're always right, and that's wrong . . . right?*

RICHARD HARRIS, *CAMELOT*, 1967

☆  ☆  ☆

Substitutions are as common in cooking as they are in Hollywood. The Oscar-winning movie *Camelot,* about King Arthur and the knights of the Round Table, was based on the highly acclaimed, long-running Broadway musical by the same name. Although the musical was a smash hit and both its leads, Richard Burton and Julie Andrews, got rave reviews, other stars were substituted for the film version.

Almost all medieval cookbooks had one form or another of frumente, a sweet whole grain pudding, usually served as a side dish to roast game. I serve it as a dessert instead and substitute the more readily available pearl barley for the coarser wheat berries suggested in the original recipe. Feel free to make substitutions of your own by adding any dried fruits you like to this rich and unusual dessert.

¾ CUP MARSALA WINE OR SWEET SHERRY

1 CUP PEARL BARLEY

1 CUP DICED MIXED DRIED FRUIT, SUCH AS CHERRIES, APRICOTS, AND APPLES

⅓ CUP SUGAR

¼ TEASPOON GROUND CINNAMON

1 CUP HEAVY CREAM

SALT

¼ CUP SLICED ALMONDS

GRATED ZEST OF 1 LEMON

1. Bring the wine to a boil over high heat in a saucepan. Stir in the barley and continue cooking until all the wine has evaporated, about 1 minute.

2. Add 3 cups of water, the dried fruit, sugar, and cinnamon and bring to a boil. Reduce the heat to low, cover, and simmer, stirring occasionally, until the barley is soft and the liquid is absorbed, about 45 minutes.

3. Add the cream and continue to simmer, stirring for 5 minutes. Remove from the heat and season to taste with salt.

4. Serve at room temperature topped with the almonds and lemon zest.

ORIGINAL RECIPE: TO MAKE FRUMENTE—Tak clene whete & braye yt wel in a morter tyl the holes gone of; sepe it til it breste in water. Nym it up & lat it cole. Tak good broth & swte mylk of kyn or of almand & tempere it therewith. Nym 3elkys of eyren rawe & saffroun & cast thereto; salt it; lat it nau3t boyle after the eyren ben cast thereinne. Messe it forth with venesoun or with fat mootoun fresch. —*THE FORME OF CURY*, 1390

—*I don't think he knows about second breakfast, Pip.*

—*What about elevenses? Luncheon? Afternoon tea?*

—DOMINIC MONAGHAN AND BILLY BOYD, *THE LORD OF THE RINGS: THE FELLOWSHIP OF THE RING*, 2001

In the Middle Ages, the main meal of the day was usually eaten at about 10 A.M.

# PEARS IN BERRY-WINE SYRUP

SERVES 4

*Nobody tosses a Dwarf!*

JOHN RHYS-DAVIES, *THE LORD OF THE RINGS: THE FELLOWSHIP OF THE RING*, 2001

☆　☆　☆

Minstrels, poets, jugglers, clowns, and dwarfs entertained at medieval feasts. Considering it is from a 1390 cookbook, this elegant dessert of wine-poached pears, perfect for your own feast, is surprisingly modern.

4 VERY FIRM PEARS, PEELED AND CORED BUT LEFT WHOLE

ONE 750-MILLILITER BOTTLE RED WINE

1 CUP SUGAR

1 PINT FRESH BLACKBERRIES OR RASPBERRIES OR FROZEN BLACKBERRIES OR RASPBERRIES, THAWED

ONE 2-INCH CINNAMON STICK

4 WHOLE CLOVES

⅛ TEASPOON GROUND CARDAMOM

1. In a saucepan large enough to hold the pears, bring the wine, sugar, berries, cinnamon stick, cloves, and cardamom to a boil over medium-high heat. Add the pears and reduce the heat to maintain a gentle simmer. Cut a circle of parchment or waxed paper slightly larger than the diameter of the saucepan and press it down into the pan until it touches the surface of the liquid. This will keep the pears submerged while they cook.

2. Cook the pears until tender, about 25 minutes. Turn off the heat and allow the pears to cool in the liquid. With a slotted spoon, transfer the pears to a plate. Remove the cinnamon stick and return the liquid to a boil over medium-high heat. Cook until very thick and syrupy, about 40 minutes. Pour the sauce through a strainer into a bowl.

3. Serve the pears topped with the warm sauce.

**ORIGINAL RECIPE: PEERES IN CONFYT**—Take peeres and pare hem clene. Take gode rede wyne & mulberries, other saundres, and seep the peeres therin, & whan thei buth ysode take hem up. Make a syryo of wyne greke, other vernage, with blaunche powdur, other white sugur and powdour ginger, & do the peres therein. Seeth it a lytel & messe it forth. —*THE FORME OF CURY,* 1390

---

*What a pity your manners don't match your looks, Your Highness.*

—ERROL FLYNN, *THE ADVENTURES OF ROBIN HOOD,* 1938

The feasting scenes from films such as *The Adventures of Robin Hood, First Knight,* and *A Knight's Tale* give us a hint about how people ate in those days. For example, as shown in the movies, no one in England used forks. Although they were common in Italy since 1071, forks were not introduced into northern Europe until the mid-1600s.

---

# MEDIEVAL FEAST

Producing a medieval feast can be great fun. The Middle Ages were such a compelling time that even the stodgiest of friends will get into the act.

To set the stage, cover the table with a heavy white tablecloth, as was done then. Picnic tables are ideal for medieval feasts because in those days tables were nothing more than wooden planks precariously balanced on sawhorses. In fact, the rule about not putting your elbows on the table started back in the Middle Ages. Tables then were so shaky that if you leaned on them, they might topple over.

The term "chairman" also comes from the Middle Ages, when only the master of the house had a proper seat. Chairs were expensive back then, so guests, if they got a seat at all, sat on simple backless benches. So feel free to use picnic benches, and if you run out of places to sit, just explain that you are only following a medieval custom, when many of the guests ate standing.

Since there was no electricity in the Middle Ages, set out lots of candles for mood and light. Use large wooden bowls filled with fruit and nuts as centerpieces.

In those days, instead of dishes, dinner was served on dried slices of bread, sort of the great-great-great-grandfather of paper plates. I love serving food that way. Not only do all the guests get a big kick out of it, but there are no plates to wash. Set the table with spoons and knives, but not forks, so guests can eat medieval-style.

In the Middle Ages, platters were set out for each course, with guests helping themselves. It was polite then to serve those seated next to you, and being asked by the host to carve the meat at your end of the table was considered a great honor. I serve dinner family-style, as was done in the Middle Ages, and set out platters, odd goblets, and candlesticks found at tag sales and thrift shops. Cast-off pewter and silver sports trophies make great serving vessels, too.

It was too risky to serve water in the Middle Ages, since it was often contaminated, so everyone—even children—drank alcoholic beverages. Beer, ale, and hard cider are all great authentic beverages to serve at your medieval feast. You might also like to make mead— honey-and-spice-flavored wine that was popular then. Just take your favorite inexpensive red or white wine and mix it with honey, a cinnamon stick, fresh ginger, cloves, cardamom, black pepper, and candied orange or lemon peel. Keep it in a closed bottle for a day or two, then strain and serve.

Besides the recipes listed in this chapter, you might like to serve other medieval favorites such as roast beef, baked ham, and stuffed chicken. Our practice of eating turkey with cranberry sauce comes from the Middle Ages, where savory meats were accompanied by tart and sweet fruit sauces. While they didn't have cranberries, a New World food, they did have other tart fruits. With your roast meats, consider serving a slow-simmered sauce of dried apricots or dried cherries cooked in honey and wine. In medieval times, chefs prepared a fantasy creature, the "cockentrice," which was a mix of gold-and-silver-gilded suckling pig and roasted capon parts. For your own modern "cockentrice," you might like to make a huge meat loaf shaped like a suckling pig with turkey legs and wings inserted at the sides. A delicious, but suckling pig–less, nod to the past.

## Movie Suggestions

*The Adventures of Marco Polo,* 1938. Story of the thirteenth-century explorer, starring Gary Cooper and Basil Rathbone.

*The Adventures of Robin Hood,* 1938. Errol Flynn, Olivia de Havilland, and Basil Rathbone star in this classic must-see.

*Becket,* 1964. Story of the relationship between the archbishop of Canterbury, Thomas à Becket, and King Henry II. Stars Richard Burton, Peter O'Toole, and John Gielgud.

*Black Knight,* 2001. Martin Lawrence is transported to fourteenth-century England.

*Braveheart,* 1995. Mel Gibson produced, directed, and stars in this story of a thirteenth-century Scotsman.

*Camelot,* 1967. Tale of King Arthur, Guinevere, and Sir Lancelot, starring Richard Harris and Vanessa Redgrave.

*A Connecticut Yankee in King Arthur's Court,* 1949. Based on Mark Twain's story of a modern man transported to the Middle Ages. Stars Bing Crosby.

*Don Quixote,* 2000. Made-for-TV movie based on the classic story by Cervantes. Stars Vanessa Williams, John Lithgow, and Isabella Rossellini.

*Dragonheart,* 1996. Dragon, Sean Connery, and knight, Dennis Quaid, join to battle tenth-century evil.

*Dragonslayer,* 1981. Wizards and fire-breathing dragons.

*Excalibur,* 1981. Story of King Arthur.

*First Knight,* 1995. Sean Connery and Richard Gere in the story of King Arthur and Sir Lancelot.

*The Flame and the Arrow,* 1950. Must-see movie starring Burt Lancaster, who did all of his own stunts in this story of an Italian Robin Hood.

*Ivanhoe,* 1952. Tale of knights and fair maidens, starring Elizabeth Taylor and Robert Taylor, no relation.

*Just Visiting,* 2001. Comedy about a medieval knight brought to the future by a sorcerer's slipup.

*A Knight in Camelot,* 1998. Whoopi Goldberg is transported to medieval England.

*Knights of the Round Table,* 1953. Robert Taylor, Ava Gardner, and Mel Ferrer in the story of King Arthur.

*A Knight's Tale,* 2001. Heath Ledger goes from squire to knight.

*The Lion in Winter,* 1968. Story of King Henry I, starring Peter O'Toole and Katharine Hepburn.

*The Lord of the Rings: The Fellowship of the Ring,* 2001. Oscar-winning fantastical story with a medieval feel. Stars Viggo Mortensen, Ian McKellen, Elijah Wood, and Sean Astin.

*The Magic Sword,* 1962. Knights, damsels in distress, sorcerers, and dragons. Stars Basil Rathbone.

*Monty Python and the Holy Grail,* 1975. Spoof of the story of King Arthur.

*The Name of the Rose,* 1986. Story of fourteenth-century Italy based on Umberto Eco's bestseller.

*Quest for Camelot,* 1998. Warner Bros. animated film about King Arthur.

*Richard III,* 1955. Shakespeare's play, directed by and starring Laurence Olivier.

*Robin Hood* movies. Besides the 1938 Errol Flynn classic, there is the 1973 animated film by Disney; the 1991 version with Kevin Costner; as well as the spoofs *The Zany Adventures of Robin Hood,* starring Morgan Fairchild, and Mel Brooks's *Robin Hood: Men in Tights.*

*The Sword in the Stone,* 1963. Disney animated film about King Arthur as a boy tutored by Merlin, the magician.

# SHAKESPEARE AND THE RENAISSANCE

### COMING ATTRACTIONS

CARAMELIZED ONION SQUARES ★ CRISP ARTICHOKE FRITTERS

SMOKED SALMON WITH WILDFLOWERS ON ENDIVE ★ HERB TART ★ SWEET RENAISSANCE PASTA

### FEATURE PRESENTATION

LAMB CHOPS WITH ALE AND DRIED FRUIT ★ CHICKEN WITH FRUIT AND WINE

SALMON IN PARCHMENT ★ RENAISSANCE RICE BALLS ★ RENAISSANCE GARDEN

### CLOSING CREDITS

FOOLPROOF GOOSEBERRY "FOOLE" ★ COURAGE TART ★ THE POPE'S CHEESECAKE

**LIGHTS, CAMERA, ACTION! ELIZABETHAN BANQUET**

MOVIE SUGGESTIONS

Michelangelo, Leonardo da Vinci, Raphael, King Henry VIII, Queen Elizabeth, and Shakespeare are just a few of the greats who lived during Renaissance and Elizabethan times. This era has sparked dozens of movies such as *The Agony and the Ecstasy, A Man for All Seasons,* and *Shakespeare in Love.*

The Renaissance, which means "the rebirth," was a time of elegance with a renewed appreciation for culture and visual beauty. Not only the art, but also the food, of this period was gorgeous. Elaborate garnishes, glorious salads, sculpted dough structures, and gold-gilded desserts adorned the tables of the rich.

Catherine de' Medici, an Italian princess, is often cited as responsible for bringing the cuisine of Renaissance Italy to France in the 1500s. She is credited with making such Italian products as artichokes, broccoli, peas, spinach, truffles, and pasta popular throughout the rest of Europe. The Italian chefs she brought with her introduced many cooking techniques into France, including working with sugar, making macaroons, and the ancient Roman method of cooking in a water bath, which the French named the bain-marie.

The recipes from this chapter come from several Italian cookbooks, including one by

Platina, written in 1474, and one by the personal chef to Pope Pius V, written in 1570. Several Elizabethan cookery books and a French cookbook by La Varenne, who is considered the father of French cuisine, contribute the rest of the dishes. I've included a few of the original recipes with misspellings and odd grammar left intact to give you a sense of the language at that time.

# CARAMELIZED ONION SQUARES

SERVES 6

*I hate it when you make me laugh, even worse when you make me cry.*

JULIA STILES, *TEN THINGS I HATE ABOUT YOU*, 1999

☆   ☆   ☆

While cooking for our first dinner party as newlyweds, I asked my brand-new spouse to help me slice onions. He bolted out of the room, never to return, I feared. Instead, inspired by the French movie *Diva,* he came back wearing a scuba mask and snorkel. I laughed until I cried, even before one onion was sliced! He's been my trusty comic relief in the kitchen ever since.

This Elizabethan sweet onion recipe is great served as a side dish or, as described here, baked on store-bought puff pastry as an appetizer. It's also terrific tossed with cooked spaghetti for a quick, inexpensive meal that will leave your guests crying for joy.

ONE 8-BY-11-INCH SHEET FROZEN PUFF PASTRY,
    THAWED
1 LARGE RED ONION, THINLY SLICED
1 LARGE VIDALIA ONION, THINLY SLICED
2 TABLESPOONS OLIVE OIL

½ CUP RAISINS
2 TABLESPOONS DARK BROWN SUGAR
2 TABLESPOONS FRUIT VINEGAR
SALT AND PEPPER
CHOPPED FRESH CHIVES

1. Preheat the oven to 400 degrees.

2. On a lightly floured work surface, roll out the puff pastry into a rectangle. Place the pastry on a baking sheet and pierce every few inches, so it does not puff up too much while baking. Bake for 15 minutes, or until golden.

3. Meanwhile, sauté the onions in the olive oil over medium-high heat until very soft, 15 minutes. Remove from the heat, stir in the raisins, brown sugar, and vinegar, and season to taste with salt and pepper.

4. Spread the onion mixture onto the cooked pastry and cut into squares.

5. Serve topped with chopped chives.

> *You can't spend the rest of your life crying. It annoys people in the movies.*
>
> —WALTER MATTHAU, *THE ODD COUPLE*, 1968
>
> The expressions "tearjerker" and "soda jerk" were both coined in America in the early 1920s.

# CRISP ARTICHOKE FRITTERS

SERVES 4

*—That . . . thing out there; at least she's fertile.*

*—She's not his wife.*

*—No, Catherine's his wife, and she's barren as a brick.*

ORSON WELLES AND PAUL SCOFIELD, *A MAN FOR ALL SEASONS*, 1966

☆　☆　☆

*A Man for All Seasons,* a movie about King Henry VIII, swept the 1966 Academy Awards, winning Oscars for Best Picture, Best Director, and Best Actor. The real King Henry VIII, notorious for having had eight wives, is credited with introducing artichokes, then thought to be aphrodisiacs, into England.

Made with frozen artichoke hearts, whose aphrodisiac qualities are still open to debate, these tasty fritters are a snap to prepare, leaving plenty of time for other passionate pursuits.

| | |
|---|---|
| ½ CUP ALL-PURPOSE FLOUR | ½ CUP MILK |
| 3 TABLESPOONS GRATED PARMESAN CHEESE | 1 LARGE EGG |
| 1½ TEASPOONS SALT | VEGETABLE OIL |
| PINCH OF PEPPER | ONE 10-OUNCE PACKAGE FROZEN ARTICHOKE |
| 1 TEASPOON DRIED PARSLEY | HEARTS, THAWED |
| PINCH OF GROUND NUTMEG | |

1. In a large bowl, combine the flour, Parmesan, salt, pepper, parsley, and nutmeg. Add the milk and egg, and using an electric mixer, blend until a smooth batter forms.

2. Pour the vegetable oil into a heavy-bottomed skillet to a depth of ½ inch and heat over medium-high heat. The oil is ready when you sprinkle a little flour into it and it sizzles.

3. Dip the artichoke hearts into the batter and gently place them in the hot oil. Fry, turning once, until golden, about 2 minutes per side.

4. Transfer to a paper-towel-lined plate to drain. Serve warm.

---

*Back home everyone said I didn't have any talent. They might be saying the same thing over here, but it sounds better in French.* —GENE KELLY, *AN AMERICAN IN PARIS*, 1951

There is a long list of foreign films about food, including such favorites as *Babette's Feast, La Grande Bouffe, Like Water for Chocolate, Eat Drink Man Woman, The Dinner Game, Tampopo,* and *A Chef in Love.*

---

# SMOKED SALMON WITH WILDFLOWERS ON ENDIVE

SERVES 8

☆　☆　☆

There were many silent films made of Shakespeare's plays, starting with *Hamlet* in 1900. *The Taming of the Shrew*, 1929, was the first Shakespeare talkie to be made, and nearly one hundred have been made since.

This modern version of a salad from Shakespeare's time is here served as an elegant finger appetizer of smoked salmon with sweet red onion relish, topped with edible flowers.

2 TABLESPOONS WHITE WINE VINEGAR

1 TABLESPOON SUGAR

1 TABLESPOON FRESHLY SQUEEZED LEMON JUICE

¼ CUP EXTRA-VIRGIN OLIVE OIL

SALT AND PEPPER

1 SMALL RED ONION, MINCED

16 ENDIVE OR OTHER LETTUCE LEAVES

2 OUNCES SMOKED SALMON, COARSELY CHOPPED

EDIBLE FLOWERS, SUCH AS CHIVE OR VIOLET PETALS

1. Place the vinegar, sugar, and lemon juice in a small bowl and slowly whisk in the olive oil. Season to taste with salt and pepper. Toss the onion in the vinaigrette and set aside for at least 1 hour to soften the onion's sharpness.

2. To assemble the appetizer, arrange the endive leaves on a serving platter. Drain the onion and place a small mound of the relish in the center of each leaf. Top with a tablespoon of the salmon and a sprinkle of flower petals.

ORIGINAL RECIPE: SALLETS FOR FISH DAYS—Salmon cut long waies with slices of onyons upon it layd and upon that to cast Violets, Oyle and Vineger. —*THE GOOD HUSWIFES JEWELL*, 1586

---

*Allow me to explain about the theater business. The natural condition is one of insurmountable obstacles on the road to imminent disaster.*

—GEOFFREY RUSH, *SHAKESPEARE IN LOVE*, 1998

Shakespeare's life and works have sparked hundreds of movies, ranging from Kenneth Branagh's *Love's Labour's Lost* to *West Side Story* and even *Ten Things I Hate About You*.

Stars such as Sarah Bernhardt, James Cagney, Mickey Rooney, Douglas Fairbanks, Mary Pickford, Elizabeth Taylor, Richard Burton, Laurence Olivier, Anthony Hopkins, Jessica Lange, Dianna Rigg, Judi Dench, Mel Gibson, Denzel Washington, Keanu Reeves, Michelle Pfeiffer, Leonardo DiCaprio, Calista Flockhart, Marlon Brando, Kate Winslet, and Kevin Kline have all appeared in Shakespeare-inspired films.

# HERB TART

SERVES 12

*Would you bargain with your pontiff?*

REX HARRISON, *THE AGONY AND THE ECSTASY*, 1965

☆  ☆  ☆

In *The Agony and the Ecstasy,* Michelangelo, played by Charlton Heston, faces imprisonment if he does not obey the pope's command to paint the Sistine Chapel. Even though the artist much prefers sculpting to painting, Michelangelo is compelled to accept the commission for the paltry fee set by the pontiff.

This recipe, created for a later Renaissance pope, combines Swiss chard, herbs, and cheese for a tasty and light first course or luncheon dish. Substitute any leafy green or even a mix of greens for the Swiss chard, if you prefer. Unlike Michelangelo, you have a choice.

2 READY-MADE 9-INCH PIECRUSTS

1 LARGE ONION, FINELY CHOPPED

2 TABLESPOONS OLIVE OIL

2 GARLIC CLOVES, MINCED

1½ POUNDS SWISS CHARD, FINELY CHOPPED

1 CUP FINELY CHOPPED MIXED FRESH HERBS, SUCH AS PARSLEY, MINT, THYME, AND BASIL

1 CUP DICED SEMISOFT CHEESE, SUCH AS TALEGGIO OR PORT SALUT

1 LARGE EGG, BEATEN

1 TEASPOON SUGAR

SALT AND PEPPER

1.  Preheat the oven to 375 degrees.

2.  Bake the piecrusts for 5 minutes and set aside.

3.  In a large pan, sauté the onion in the olive oil over medium heat for 10 minutes. Add the garlic and cook for 1 minute. Raise the heat, add the Swiss chard and herbs, and cook until just wilted, less than a minute. Remove the pan from the heat, add the cheese, egg, and sugar, and mix well. Season to taste with salt and pepper. Pour the mixture into the piecrusts and bake for 30 minutes, or until set.

# SWEET RENAISSANCE PASTA

SERVES 6

*I must think of something quickly because before you know it,*
*the Renaissance will be here and we'll all be painting.*
WOODY ALLEN, *EVERYTHING YOU ALWAYS WANTED TO KNOW ABOUT SEX (BUT WERE AFRAID TO ASK)*, 1972

☆ ☆ ☆

Tomatoes, a New World food, were not introduced into Europe until after Columbus. Later, tomatoes were made into a sauce for roast meats but during the Renaissance were never eaten with pasta. During that period, pasta was served with sweet sauces like this unforgettable blend of wine, spices, and prunes. Also great made with dried figs, this easy-to-prepare recipe creates a gourmet first course with little effort.

2 CUPS RED WINE

9 OUNCES PRUNES, PITTED AND CHOPPED

3 TABLESPOONS SUGAR

2 TABLESPOONS MINCED FRESH GINGER

SALT AND PEPPER

1 POUND PASTA (ANY TYPE)

2 SHALLOTS, MINCED

4 TABLESPOONS (½ STICK) BUTTER, CUT INTO CHUNKS

DASH OF PARMESAN CHEESE

DASH OF GROUND NUTMEG

1. Place the wine, prunes, sugar, and ginger in a saucepan and bring to a low boil over medium heat. Reduce heat and simmer until most of the wine evaporates, about 20 minutes. Allow to cool slightly and puree in a food processor until smooth. Season to taste with salt and pepper.

2. Meanwhile, cook the pasta according to package directions. Drain and place the pasta in a serving bowl with the shallots and butter. Stir until the butter is melted. Toss with the prune sauce and top with the Parmesan and nutmeg.

# LAMB CHOPS WITH ALE AND DRIED FRUIT

SERVES 6

*—Strangely enough, it all turns out well.*

*—How?*

*—I don't know. It's a mystery.*

GEOFFREY RUSH AND TOM WILKINSON, *SHAKESPEARE IN LOVE,* 1998

☆　☆　☆

This recipe is one of my favorite Elizabethan dishes. You just toss all the ingredients into a roasting pan and strangely enough, in just half an hour, it becomes a gourmet meal. It's a mystery.

2 LARGE ONIONS, THINLY SLICED

3 FRESH ROSEMARY SPRIGS

4 FRESH THYME SPRIGS

¼ CUP CHOPPED FRESH PARSLEY

½ TEASPOON GROUND CINNAMON

½ TEASPOON GROUND GINGER

½ TEASPOON GROUND NUTMEG

4 WHOLE CLOVES

12 LOIN LAMB CHOPS, ABOUT 7 OUNCES EACH

SALT AND PEPPER

8 LARGE PRUNES, PITTED AND HALVED

4 DRIED APRICOTS

¼ CUP RAISINS

10 DATES, PITTED AND HALVED

12 OUNCES ALE OR BEER

1. Preheat the oven to 375 degrees.

2. Lay the onion slices on the bottom of a dry nonstick baking pan. Distribute the rosemary, thyme, parsley, cinnamon, ginger, nutmeg, and cloves over the onion. Season the lamb chops with salt and pepper and lay in a single layer over the herbs. Scatter the prunes, apricots, raisins, and dates over the chops and pour on the ale. Cover tightly with aluminum foil and bake for 30 minutes, or until the chops are medium.

3. Preheat the broiler.

4. Remove the aluminum foil from the pan and broil for 2 to 3 minutes, until the lamb chops are browned.

5. Spoon the onions and fruit onto the center of a serving platter and top with the lamb chops. Drizzle the cooking juices over the chops.

ORIGINAL RECIPE: TO MAKE STEWED STEAKS — Take a peece of Mutton and cut it in peeces, and wash it verie cleane, and put it into a faire pot with Ale, or with half wine, then make it boyle, and skumme it cleane, and put into your pot a faggot of rosemarie and time: then take some parsely picked fine, and some onions cut round, and let them all boyle together, then take prunes, & reasons, dates and currants, and let it boyle altogether, and season it with Sinamon and ginger, Nutmegs, two or three Cloves, and Salt, and so serve it on soppes, and garnish it with fruite. — *THE GOOD HUSWIFES JEWELL*, 1586

---

*Oh, stage love will never be true love while the law of the land has our heroines played by pip-squeak boys in petticoats.* — GWYNETH PALTROW, *SHAKESPEARE IN LOVE*, 1998

Although they were allowed to act in Italy, women in England were forbidden by law to perform as actors on the stage. Instead, boys and young men played all the female parts.

---

# CHICKEN WITH FRUIT AND WINE

SERVES 4

*To be or not to be, that is the question.*

MEL GIBSON, *HAMLET*, 1990

☆　☆　☆

Gold, commonly prescribed to cure all sorts of ills, was thought to restore youth and vigor and was often included as an ingredient in recipes such as this one from Shakespeare's England. This modern version omits the gold but keeps all the other rich Elizabethan flavors.

4 CHICKEN LEGS AND THIGHS (ABOUT 2 POUNDS), SEPARATED

SALT AND PEPPER

¼ CUP ALL-PURPOSE FLOUR

1 TABLESPOON OLIVE OIL

2 CUPS WHITE WINE

¼ CUP CURRANTS

½ CUP CHOPPED PITTED PRUNES

½ CUP CHOPPED PITTED DATES

1 TABLESPOON MINCED FRESH GINGER

½ TEASPOON GROUND NUTMEG

PINCH OF GROUND CINNAMON

1 TART APPLE, PEELED, CORED, AND SLICED

1. Sprinkle the chicken with salt and pepper and the flour. Heat the olive oil in large nonstick pan over high heat and brown the chicken on all sides. Remove the chicken from the pan. Add the wine, stir to loosen the brown bits, and bring to a boil. Add the currants, prunes, dates, ginger, nutmeg, and cinnamon. Return the chicken to the pan, cover with a tight lid, and reduce to low heat. Simmer, stirring occasionally, until the chicken is very tender, about 30 minutes.

2. Remove the chicken from the pan, place on a serving platter, and cover to keep warm. Add the apple slices to the pan liquid and simmer until the apple is soft and the liquid is reduced by half, about 8 minutes. Pour the sauce over the chicken and serve.

ORIGINAL RECIPE: TO STEW A COCKE — You must cutte him in five pieces and washe him cleane and take Prunes, currants and dates, cutte very small and Raysins of the Sunne, and Sugar beaten very small, Cynamon, Ginger and nutmeggs likewise beaten, and a little Maydens cutte very small, and you must put him in a pipkin, and put in almost a pint of Muskadine, and then your spice and sugar uppon your Cocke, and put in your fruite betweene every quarter, and a peece of Golde betweene every peece of your Cocke, then you must make a lidde of Wood to fit for your pipkin, and close it as close as you can with paste, that no ayre come out, nor water can come in. — *THE GOOD HUSWIFES JEWELL*, 1586

# SALMON IN PARCHMENT

SERVES 6

*I'm having fish tonight!!*
BARRY HUMPHRIES, *FINDING NEMO*, 2003

☆　☆　☆

Fish pies were often molded into the shape of the fish being eaten and were decorated with elaborate pastry scales, fins, claws, and gills. For an easier-to-prepare version, here the salmon and all the interesting Elizabethan ingredients are wrapped in a piece of cooking parchment. I sometimes draw a cartoony fish on the parchment before baking for a humorous nod to the more elaborate olden-day decorations.

6 SHEETS PARCHMENT PAPER (ABOUT 8 INCHES
    BY 8 INCHES EACH)
OLIVE OIL
ONE 13-OUNCE CAN ARTICHOKE HEARTS,
    DRAINED AND CUT INTO QUARTERS
6 SKINLESS SALMON FILLETS (ABOUT 7 OUNCES
    EACH)
SALT AND PEPPER

½ TEASPOON GROUND NUTMEG
¼ CUP COARSELY CHOPPED PISTACHIO NUTS
ONE 4-OUNCE CAN SMOKED OYSTERS, DRAINED
1 SMALL BUNCH ASPARAGUS, ENDS REMOVED,
    CUT INTO 1-INCH PIECES
16 GREEN SEEDLESS GRAPES, HALVED
JUICE OF 1 LEMON
LEMON WEDGES

1. Preheat the oven to 375 degrees.

2. Place the parchment sheets on a work surface and drizzle with olive oil. Divide the artichoke hearts among the 6 sheets, placing them in a straight line down the center of each.

3. Season both sides of the salmon fillets with salt and pepper and the nutmeg. Place the pistachios on a plate and press both sides of each fillet into the nuts. Put a nut-coated fillet over the artichokes on each sheet and scatter the oysters, asparagus, and grapes over and around the fillets. Top with the lemon juice and a drizzle of olive oil and seal, tucking the ends under the fish. Place on a baking sheet and bake for 20 to 25 minutes, until the fish is cooked through.

4. Serve in the parchment with lemon wedges.

# RENAISSANCE RICE BALLS

SERVES 10

*Whoever said orange was the new pink was seriously disturbed.*

REESE WITHERSPOON, *LEGALLY BLONDE*, 2001

☆   ☆   ☆

Rice balls like these, called *arancini,* or little oranges, are still made in many parts of Italy. During the Renaissance, these savory balls would have been colored purple or orange with dried edible flower petals or saffron. You can easily re-create the effect using food coloring, but they are just as delicious without it!

1 POUND ARBORIO RICE

⅓ CUP HEAVY CREAM

1 LARGE EGG, BEATEN

1 CUP GRATED CACCIOCAVALLO OR PARMESAN
   CHEESE

2 TABLESPOONS SUGAR

YELLOW FOOD COLORING (OPTIONAL)

PURPLE FOOD COLORING (OPTIONAL)

½ CUP ALL-PURPOSE FLOUR OR DRIED BREAD
   CRUMBS

¾ CUP VEGETABLE OIL

1. Cook the rice according to package directions. Combine the cooked rice, cream, egg, cacciocavallo, and sugar in a large bowl. Cover and refrigerate until thoroughly chilled.

2. If desired, divide the rice into 3 equal portions. Using the food coloring, color 1 part bright yellow, 1 purple, and leave the remaining white.

3. Form the rice into 1-inch balls.

4. Place the flour on a flat plate. Heat 3 to 4 tablespoons of the vegetable oil in a skillet over medium-high heat. Lightly roll 1 color of the rice balls in the flour. Cook, turning occasionally, until completely browned on all sides. Remove the rice balls from the pan and drain on paper towels. Discard the oil in the pan, wipe it clean, and repeat the process with the remaining 2 batches of rice balls.

---

*Secret's in the sauce.* —CICELY TYSON, *FRIED GREEN TOMATOES*, 1991

There are lots of film titles that contain food words. Here are just a few of my favorites, not just for the titles, but for the wonderful stories these movies tell: *Chocolat, Good Burger, Fried Green Tomatoes, Home Fries, My Dinner with Andre, Soul Food,* and *Tortilla Soup.*

---

# RENAISSANCE GARDEN

SERVES 6

*The secret of acting is sincerity—*
*and if you can fake that, you've got it made.*

GEORGE BURNS

☆　☆　☆

Guests will swear you spent hours in the kitchen to prepare this impressive dish. In fact, this elaborate-looking salad of baby greens topped with colorful assorted dried fruit and garnished with tall rosemary branches stuck in lemon halves takes only minutes to assemble. Very dramatic. Very delicious. Very easy. So go ahead, fake it.

| | |
|---|---|
| ¼ CUP RED WINE VINEGAR | 4 LONG, STURDY FRESH ROSEMARY BRANCHES |
| ¼ CUP EXTRA-VIRGIN OLIVE OIL | 2 LARGE LEMONS, HALVED |
| 2 TEASPOONS LIGHT BROWN SUGAR | 8 CANDIED OR FRESH WHOLE CHERRY PAIRS |
| SALT AND PEPPER | 1 CUP READY-MADE CROUTONS |
| ¼ CUP RAISINS | 6 CUPS BABY SALAD GREENS |
| 8 DATES, PITTED AND SLICED | ½ CUP SLICED ALMONDS |
| 6 DRIED FIGS, SLICED | ¼ CUP CAPERS, DRAINED |

1. Whisk together the vinegar, olive oil, and brown sugar in a bowl. Season to taste with salt and pepper. Stir in the raisins, dates, and figs and allow to rest, to soften the dried fruit, while you prepare the rest of the salad.

2. Press 1 of the rosemary branches into the rounded end of each lemon half. Using the stems, drape 2 cherry pairs onto each rosemary branch.

3. To assemble the salad, put the croutons in a mound in the center of a large serving platter, to give the salad added height in the middle. Scatter the salad greens over the croutons and around the platter. Stir the vinaigrette with the dried fruit and pour evenly over the salad. Sprinkle the almonds and capers over the top. Place the rosemary branches on the four sides of the platter and serve.

# FOOLPROOF GOOSEBERRY "FOOLE"

SERVES 4

*Life's a banquet and most poor suckers are starving to death!*

ROSALIND RUSSELL, *AUNTIE MAME*, 1958

☆  ☆  ☆

"Foole" is a classic Elizabethan banquet dessert of whipped cream with sweetened berries. If you can't find gooseberries, try substituting a slightly tart dried fruit such as apricots or crab apples. Guests will love this delicately delicious end to your Renaissance banquet.

6 OUNCES GOOSEBERRIES

3 TABLESPOONS GRANULATED SUGAR

PINCH OF GROUND NUTMEG

1 CUP HEAVY CREAM

1 TABLESPOON LIGHT BROWN SUGAR

1. Place the gooseberries, granulated sugar, and nutmeg in a small saucepan with 1 cup of water and simmer over low heat for 15 minutes. Discard any loose skins and mash the berries with a fork. Allow to cool to room temperature.

2. Whip the cream with an electric mixer until soft peaks form.

3. Divide the whipped cream among 4 small serving glasses and gently stir in the fruit mixture. Sprinkle with the brown sugar and serve immediately.

# COURAGE TART

SERVES 8

*It's as if my quill is broken.*

JOSEPH FIENNES, *SHAKESPEARE IN LOVE*, 1998

☆   ☆   ☆

This recipe, from a 1587 English cookbook, promised to give "courage to a man or woman." "Courage" was the polite word for sexual virility, so the recipe included sweet potatoes and wine, considered aphrodisiacs then. A sort of Elizabethan Viagra.

1 LARGE SWEET POTATO, PEELED AND DICED

2 CUPS WHITE DESSERT WINE, SUCH AS
    MUSCATEL

2 APPLES, PEELED, CORED, AND DICED

3 DATES, PITTED AND CHOPPED

2 TABLESPOONS LIGHT BROWN SUGAR

⅛ TEASPOON GROUND CINNAMON

⅛ TEASPOON GROUND GINGER

PINCH OF GROUND CLOVES

2 TABLESPOONS BUTTER

4 LARGE EGG YOLKS

2 LARGE EGG WHITES

1 READY-MADE 9-INCH DEEP-DISH PIECRUST

1. Preheat the oven to 350 degrees.

2. Place the sweet potato and wine in a large saucepan over medium heat and simmer for 10 minutes. Add the apples and dates and simmer until both are tender, about 10 minutes. Allow to cool slightly and puree in a food processor until smooth. Add the brown sugar, cinnamon, ginger, cloves, butter, and egg yolks and puree until well combined.

3. In a large bowl, using an electric mixer, beat the egg whites to soft peaks. Gently fold the sweet potato mixture into the egg whites. Pour the filling into the piecrust and bake for 1 hour, or until the center springs back when pressed.

# THE POPE'S CHEESECAKE

SERVES 10

*Michelangelo will paint the ceiling. He will paint the ceiling or hang.*

REX HARRISON, *THE AGONY AND THE ECSTASY*, 1965

☆　☆　☆

*The Agony and the Ecstasy* is about the creation of the Sistine Chapel, a project dreaded by Michelangelo, who favored sculpting over painting.

This Italian Renaissance recipe was a particular favorite of Pope Julius III, the pontiff who hired Michelangelo as chief architect of Saint Peter's Basilica, a job Michelangelo, then in his seventies, thoroughly enjoyed. You and your guests will certainly enjoy this light cheesecake delicately flavored with apples.

1½ POUNDS WHOLE MILK RICOTTA CHEESE

4 LARGE EGGS

½ CUP HEAVY CREAM

¾ CUP SUGAR

½ CUP APPLESAUCE

½ CUP SEMOLINA FLOUR

2 CUPS APPLE JUICE

3 TABLESPOONS CONFECTIONERS' SUGAR

4 DROPS ROSE WATER (OPTIONAL)

1. Preheat the oven to 350 degrees. Generously grease a 10-inch springform pan and set aside.

2. In a large bowl, using an electric mixer, combine the ricotta, eggs, and cream until very smooth. Add the sugar, applesauce, and flour and beat until well blended. Pour into the prepared pan and bake for 1 hour, or until the cheesecake is set and light golden on top. Allow the cake to cool completely in the pan before unmolding and glazing.

3. Meanwhile, bring the apple juice to a boil in a saucepan over medium-high heat. Cook until the juice is reduced to a thick syrup, about 15 minutes. Allow to cool, then whisk in the confectioners' sugar and rose water, if using, until smooth.

4. Spread the glaze over the top of the cooled cheesecake. Slice and serve.

# ELIZABETHAN BANQUET

During the Renaissance and Elizabethan times, nobles held banquets so they could build alliances with neighboring noblemen, show off, and repay courtesies. If the banquet was for the townspeople, a general notice was posted in the central square. If it was a smaller affair, messengers were sent house-to-house to deliver personal invitations.

For your own Elizabethan banquet, you might want to write invitations in calligraphy or use a fancy script font from your computer. I like to use language of the time, so I often quote Shakespeare in my invitations. Lines such as "Revel and feast it at my house," from *The Comedy of Errors,* or "Give me your hand. We must needs dine together," from *Timon of Athens,* work well. I seal the envelope with wax, as was done back then.

Use dramatic Renaissance colors such as deep gold, rich burgundy, royal blue, and dark green or purple for the tablecloth, napkins, and candles. In those days, a page offered arriving guests a bowl of water scented with flower petals in which to wash their hands. A nice touch to your own banquet might be to place bowls of scented water with flower petals in the guest bathroom.

Gold, thought to be a cure-all and to restore youth, was a common ingredient in

Renaissance dishes. All sorts of roast meats and desserts were decorated with real gold, which, by the way, is totally harmless to eat. Gold was so prized that sauces were made yellow with saffron or onion skins. For fun, I like to serve at least one dish surrounded by "gold" and use foil-wrapped chocolate coins or gold-toned silver dollars.

During the Renaissance, dinner guests often read poems or told riddles and jokes during dinner. Encourage your guests to do the same. You might like to print out some of your favorite Shakespeare sonnets or passages for them to read out loud during dinner.

Dessert during Renaissance and Elizabethan times was served away from the dinner table in another room, often in an outside gazebo. The dessert course was called the banquet in those days. Nowadays, of course, "banquet" has come to mean the same thing as "feast," but then, dinner was called a feast, dessert a banquet. The dessert plates were often decorated with jokes, puns, or inspirational sayings. For your banquet dessert course, you might want to create your own decorated plates by writing a movie quote on each plate, using a tube of icing gel. Guests have to guess what movie it's from, or no dessert!

## Movie Suggestions

*The Agony and the Ecstasy,* 1965. Story of Michelangelo's painting of the Sistine Chapel, starring Charlton Heston.

*Dangerous Beauty,* 1998. Sixteenth-century Venetian beauty becomes a courtesan.

*Elizabeth,* 1998. Cate Blanchett, Geoffrey Rush, and Joseph Fiennes star in the story of Queen Elizabeth I.

*Hamlet.* Versions include the 1948 Oscar-winning version with Laurence Olivier; 1990, with Mel Gibson; 1996, with Kenneth Branagh; and 2000, with Ethan Hawke.

*Henry V,* 1989. Shakespeare's play, directed by and starring Kenneth Branagh.

*Highlander,* 1986. An immortal sixteenth-century Scotsman battles evil. Stars Christopher Lambert and Sean Connery.

*If I Were King,* 1938. Ronald Colman as a fifteenth-century good guy battling bad guy King Louis XI, played by Basil Rathbone.

*Joan of Arc,* 1999. Fifteenth-century heroine played by Leelee Sobieski, also starring Peter O'Toole, Shirley MacLaine, and Olympia Dukakis.

*A Man for All Seasons,* 1966. Story of Henry VIII, starring Paul Scofield, Orson Welles, and John Hurt. It was also remade in 1988, directed by and starring Charlton Heston.

*Mary, Queen of Scots,* 1971. Tale of Queen Elizabeth's cousin. Stars Vanessa Redgrave and Glenda Jackson.

*The Messenger: The Story of Joan of Arc,* 1999. Young martyr played by Milla Jovovich, starring John Malkovich, Dustin Hoffman, and Faye Dunaway.

*Orlando,* 1992. Based on Virginia Woolf's novel about a 400-year-old Englishman who evolves into a woman.

*The Prince and the Pauper.* Mark Twain's classic story of trading places was made in 1937, with Errol Flynn; in 1962, with Guy Williams; in 1978, with Oliver Reed and Raquel Welch; and in 2000, with twins Jonathan and Robert Timmins.

*Romeo and Juliet,* 1968. Olivia Hussey, age fifteen, stars. She is close to the age of Shakespeare's Juliet, who was fourteen.

*Shakespeare in Love,* 1998. Stars Joseph Fiennes as the Bard and Gwyneth Paltrow as his love.

*The Taming of the Shrew,* 1967. Stars Elizabeth Taylor and Richard Burton.

*The Virgin Queen,* 1955. Story of the relationship between Queen Elizabeth I and Sir Walter Raleigh, starring Bette Davis, Richard Todd, and Joan Collins.

# AMERICA'S EARLY YEARS

### COMING ATTRACTIONS
HAM-STUFFED TOMATOES ★ HOECAKES WITH MAPLE BUTTER ★ NATIVE AMERICAN PEANUT SOUP

### FEATURE PRESENTATION
OLD-FASHIONED SOUTHERN FRIED CHICKEN WITH GRAVY ★ CHICKEN JAMBALAYA
SUCCOTASH ★ CORN FRITTERS ★ BUTTERMILK BISCUITS

### CLOSING CREDITS
PEANUT "COFFEE" ★ SUGAR CRISPS WITH CHOCOLATE DIPPING SAUCE
BOURBON SWEET POTATO PIE ★ SOUTHERN PEACH ICE CREAM

### LIGHTS, CAMERA, ACTION! ALL-AMERICAN PICNIC
MOVIE SUGGESTIONS

America's early years, the time of our first settlers, our fight for independence, and the conflict between the North and South, have been depicted in films such as *Gone with the Wind* and *The Patriot*. This was a time of pioneers, a rough-and-ready lot, who had to make due with the ingredients at hand, often improvising to provide nourishing meals. Distinctly different from the gourmet meals served by European nobility, the food of America's early years reflects wholesome simplicity, meals that could feed many and be prepared without fuss.

The menu for this chapter includes a range of classic American dishes such as old-fashioned southern fried chicken, buttermilk biscuits, and succotash. Recipes come from three important historical cookbooks: *American Cookery,* the very first cookbook published in America; *What Mrs. Fisher Knows About Old Southern Cooking,* the first cookbook written by an African American; and *The Virginia House-wife,* America's first regional cookbook. To give you a taste of how recipes were written back then, I've included a few of them from these significant cookbooks.

This menu is perfect for a picnic, as almost all the dishes can be made in advance and eaten at room temperature.

# HAM-STUFFED TOMATOES

SERVES 4

*I'm going to live through this, and when it's all over,*

*I'll never be hungry again!*

VIVIEN LEIGH, *GONE WITH THE WIND*, 1939

☆  ☆  ☆

Many actresses were considered for the starring role in *Gone with the Wind,* the movie based on Margaret Mitchell's bestselling novel, including Tallulah Bankhead, Joan Crawford, Bette Davis, Jean Harlow, Katharine Hepburn, Carole Lombard, and Loretta Young.

This great appetizer from a Civil War cookbook is perfect with epics about the era, such as *Glory, Gettysburg,* and *The Red Badge of Courage.*

5 TOMATOES

4 OUNCES HAM, FINELY CHOPPED

24 SALTINE CRACKERS, CRUSHED (ABOUT 1 CUP)

2 TABLESPOONS BUTTER, MELTED

2 TEASPOONS CHOPPED FRESH PARSLEY

SALT AND PEPPER

1. Preheat the oven to 375 degrees.

2. Cut about ¼ inch off the tops of 4 of the tomatoes. Reserve. Using a spoon, scoop out the centers and discard. Set aside the 4 hollow tomatoes.

3. Coarsely chop the remaining 1 tomato and put into a bowl. Add the ham, crackers, butter, and parsley and stir to mix well. Season to taste with salt and pepper.

4. Season the tomato cavities with salt and pepper. Divide the stuffing mixture among the tomatoes, packing it firmly into each. Place in a lightly buttered baking dish.

5. Bake for 20 minutes, or until the tomatoes are soft and the filling is browned. Serve warm, garnished with the tops resting on the edges of the tomatoes.

*I was a stand-up tomato: a juicy, sexy, beefsteak tomato! Nobody does vegetables like me!*

—DUSTIN HOFFMAN, *TOOTSIE*, 1982

None of the first English colonists had ever tasted tomatoes before arriving in America. Tomatoes, a New World vegetable, were introduced into Europe by Spanish explorers in the 1500s. At first, they were believed to be poisonous and were used only as decorative plants. When the Europeans finally got around to eating them, they thought tomatoes were aphrodisiacs and called them love apples. Their aphrodisiac connection is why Americans use the slang "tomato" for a sexy woman.

# HOECAKES WITH MAPLE BUTTER

SERVES 6

*Why should I agree to swap one tyrant three thousand miles away*
*for three thousand tyrants one mile away?*

MEL GIBSON, *THE PATRIOT*, 2000

☆   ☆   ☆

Hoecakes got their name because they were made in the field over an open fire on the flat end of a garden hoe. This recipe for sweet corn griddle cakes comes from the first cookbook written by an American, *American Cookery* by Amelia Simmons (1796). Hers was the first to mention ingredients indigenous to America, such as corn, cranberries, maple syrup, and watermelon, which Simmons called "the American citron."

A perfect starter or side dish, hoecakes are great for brunch, too.

| | |
|---|---|
| ½ CUP MILK | ½ TEASPOON SALT |
| 2 LARGE EGGS | PEANUT OR VEGETABLE OIL |
| 2 TABLESPOONS LIGHT MOLASSES | 4 TABLESPOONS (½ STICK) BUTTER, SOFTENED |
| 1 CUP CORNMEAL | 2 TABLESPOONS PURE MAPLE SYRUP |
| 2 TABLESPOONS ALL-PURPOSE FLOUR | |

1. In a large bowl, whisk together the milk, eggs, and molasses. Add the cornmeal, flour, and salt and whisk until very smooth.

2. Heat about 1 teaspoon of peanut oil in a nonstick skillet or griddle over medium heat. Drop a tablespoonful of the batter into the hot pan (the hoecakes are small). Cook until browned, about 1 minute, then flip and cook the other side. Continue with the remaining batter, adding more oil as needed.

3. Meanwhile, make the maple butter. Using a fork or whisk, whip the butter and syrup together until fluffy.

4. Serve the hoecakes warm in a napkin-lined basket with the maple butter on the side.

ORIGINAL RECIPE: JOHNY [*SIC*] CAKE, OR HOE CAKE—Scald 1 pint of milk and put to 3 pints of Indian meal, and half pint of flour—bake before the fire. Or scald with milk two thirds of the Indian meal, or wet two thirds with boiling water, add salt, molasses and shortening, work up with cold water pretty still, and bake as above.

—*AMERICAN COOKERY*, 1796

*I'm a parent. I haven't got the luxury of principles.* —MEL GIBSON, *THE PATRIOT*, 2000

In *The Patriot,* Mel Gibson plays a widower-father reluctantly thrust into the Revolution when a British soldier kills his son. Although the script initially called for Gibson's character to have six children, he added another to reflect his real-life family of seven.

# NATIVE AMERICAN PEANUT SOUP

SERVES 8

*I used to be able to name every nut there was.*

CHRISTOPHER GUEST, *BEST IN SHOW*, 2000

☆　☆　☆

Native Americans called peanuts "groundnuts" because they grew close to the soil, unlike other nuts, which came from trees. This peanut soup is also outstanding made with pecans or hickory nuts, America's other indigenous nuts.

1 LARGE ONION, CHOPPED

2 TABLESPOONS PEANUT OR VEGETABLE OIL

1 LARGE SWEET POTATO, PEELED AND CUBED

1 CUP UNSALTED PEANUTS, PLUS MORE FOR
    GARNISH

¼ CUP CREAMY PEANUT BUTTER

½ TEASPOON GROUND CUMIN

½ TEASPOON GROUND CORIANDER

¼ TEASPOON GROUND CARDAMOM

6 CUPS CHICKEN OR VEGETABLE STOCK, OR
    WATER

JUICE AND GRATED ZEST OF 1 LIME

SALT AND PEPPER

CAYENNE PEPPER

CHOPPED FRESH CILANTRO

1. Sauté the onion in the peanut oil in a large, heavy-bottomed saucepan over medium heat until golden, about 10 minutes. Stir in the sweet potato, peanuts, peanut butter, cumin, coriander, cardamom, and stock and bring to a boil. Cover and cook until the sweet potatoes are very soft, about 30 minutes.

2. Working in small batches, puree the soup in a blender and transfer to a large saucepan. Stir in the lime juice and add salt, pepper, and cayenne to taste.

3. To serve, ladle the soup into bowls and garnish with the lime zest, cilantro, and chopped peanuts.

# OLD-FASHIONED SOUTHERN FRIED CHICKEN WITH GRAVY

SERVES 4

*I work at Kentucky Fried Chicken.*
*I sell biscuits and gravy all over the Southlands.*

JOHN CUSACK, *GROSSE POINTE BLANK*, 1997

☆　☆　☆

This recipe for crispy fried chicken is from *What Mrs. Fisher Knows About Old Southern Cooking,* the first cookbook published by an African American. Abby Fisher, an ex-slave who won many awards for her pies and canned goods at various state fairs, published her book in 1881.

Hot buttery biscuits dipped in honey or gravy, as well as corn on the cob—which Mrs. Fisher recommends boiling in salted water for precisely seven minutes—were the typical southern accompaniments to fried chicken.

1 FRYING CHICKEN (ABOUT 4 POUNDS), CUT INTO SERVING PIECES

SALT AND PEPPER

1 TEASPOON CAYENNE PEPPER

1½ CUPS SELF-RISING FLOUR, PLUS MORE AS NEEDED

PEANUT OR VEGETABLE OIL

⅓ CUP CHICKEN STOCK

1. Place several ice cubes in a bowl of cold water and soak the chicken for 5 to 10 minutes. Pat dry and liberally season with salt and pepper.

2. Put the cayenne and flour into a large bowl and add salt and pepper. Roll each piece of chicken in the flour.

3. Fill a heavy-bottomed skillet with peanut oil to a depth of about ¾ inch. Heat the oil over high heat until hot but not smoking. Put the dark-meat chicken pieces into the skillet first, as they take longer to cook than white meat. Put the pieces into the hot skillet one at a time, slowly, so that the oil temperature doesn't drop. After the dark meat has been cooking for about 5 minutes, slowly add the white-meat pieces. Brown the chicken well on one side before turning, about 8 minutes per side.

4. Remove the cooked chicken pieces and place on absorbent paper.

5. Pour off all but 2 tablespoons of the peanut oil, add 1 tablespoon of the flour, and stir well over a low flame. Gradually add the chicken stock and continue stirring until smooth. Season to taste with salt and pepper and serve on the side.

ORIGINAL RECIPE: FRIED CHICKEN—Cut the chicken up, separating every joint, and wash clean. Salt and pepper it, and roll into flour well. Have your fat very hot, and drop the pieces into it, and then cook brown. The chicken is done when the fork passes easily into it. After the chicken is all cooked, leave a little of the hot fat in the skillet; then take a tablespoon of dry flour and brown it in the fat, stirring it around, then pour water in and stir till the gravy is as thin as soup. —*WHAT MRS. FISHER KNOWS ABOUT OLD SOUTHERN COOKING,* 1881

*I ain't fightin' this war for you, sir.* —DENZEL WASHINGTON, *GLORY,* 1989

Denzel Washington, the second African American awarded an Oscar for Best Supporting Actor, won for his role as Private Trip in *Glory,* the story of the first all-black volunteer troop in the Civil War. Led by Colonel Robert Shaw, played by Matthew Broderick—a distant relative of the real Robert Shaw—this Fifty-fourth Regiment proved that blacks were brave, disciplined soldiers.

Hattie McDaniel, in 1940, was the first African-American actress to win an Academy Award for her supporting role in *Gone with the Wind.*

In 1964, Sidney Poitier was the first African American to win an Academy Award for Best Actor, for his role in *Lilies of the Field.*

In 1983, Louis Gossett Jr. became the first African American to win the Oscar for Best Supporting Actor, for his role in *An Officer and a Gentleman.*

Halle Berry became the first African American to win a Best Actress Oscar in 2002, for her role in *Monster's Ball.*

# CHICKEN JAMBALAYA

SERVES 8

*Give us free. Give us free. Give us free.*

DJIMON HOUNSOU, *AMISTAD*, 1997

☆   ☆   ☆

Jambalaya, a Creole dish, is a mixture of the cuisines of the Caribbean and Africa, with a heavy Spanish influence. This make-ahead crowd-pleaser comes from an 1881 cookbook and is the first published recipe for jambalaya.

I like the original directions to season "high with pepper," but to please all sorts of palates, I serve it with tiny bowls of red pepper flakes and cayenne on the side so everyone can adjust the heat to their own liking.

| | |
|---|---|
| 1 LARGE VIDALIA ONION, DICED | 1½ CUPS CONVERTED WHITE RICE |
| 2 TABLESPOONS PEANUT OR VEGETABLE OIL | 1½ CUPS DICED HAM |
| 2 TO 3 LARGE GARLIC CLOVES, MINCED | 1 TEASPOON RED PEPPER FLAKES |
| 4 BONELESS, SKINLESS CHICKEN BREASTS | TWO 28-OUNCE CANS DICED TOMATOES |
| (ABOUT 6 OUNCES EACH), CUT INTO STRIPS | 6 SCALLIONS, WHITE PARTS ONLY, DICED |
| SALT AND PEPPER | |

1. In a large, heavy-bottomed pot, sauté the onion in the peanut oil over medium heat until soft, about 5 minutes. Add the garlic and continue cooking for another minute or two.

2. Season the chicken liberally with salt and pepper and add to the pot. Sauté for 2 to 3 minutes. Stir in the rice, ham, red pepper flakes, and tomatoes. Cover and simmer on low until the rice is tender, about 30 minutes. Remove from the heat.

3. Stir in the scallions and season to taste with salt and pepper. Serve warm.

---

*I had a farm in Africa at the foot of the Ngong Hills.* —MERYL STREEP, *OUT OF AFRICA*, 1985

Many of America's favorite ingredients, such as coffee, okra, eggplant, and black-eyed peas, were brought to the New World from Africa. We associate rice with the Carolinas, but rice, too, came to America from Africa.

# SUCCOTASH

SERVES 8

*Truth is a very valuable thing and I believe we should be a little economical with it.*

FREDRIC MARCH, *THE ADVENTURES OF MARK TWAIN*, 1944

☆　☆　☆

While traveling in Europe in 1878, Mark Twain, who hated foreign food, wrote home rhapsodizing about the dozens and dozens of American dishes he longed for, including succotash.

Succotash, a stew of corn and beans, is a Native American creation, often containing pumpkin and other ingredients. If you like, add walnuts to this delicious side dish, as was done by the Cherokees.

1 PURPLE ONION, DICED

6 OUNCES CANADIAN-STYLE BACON, DICED

2 TABLESPOONS BUTTER

1 PINT CHERRY TOMATOES, HALVED

1½ CUPS LIMA BEANS

1½ CUPS CORN KERNELS

SALT AND PEPPER

½ CUP CHOPPED WALNUTS (OPTIONAL)

Sauté the onion and Canadian bacon in the butter over medium heat until the onion is soft, about 5 minutes. Add the tomatoes and cook until softened, 4 to 5 minutes. Add the lima beans and corn and simmer until tender, about 5 minutes. Season to taste with salt and pepper and top with the walnuts, if using. Serve hot.

ORIGINAL RECIPE: CIRCUIT HASH—One dozen tomatoes, one quart of butter beans, one dozen ears of corn cut off from cob, quarter pound of lean and fat pork cut in fine pieces, if pork is not liked, use two tablespoonfuls of butter; put on in a saucepan and stew one hour. Note. Five minutes before dinner put in the corn to cook with the rest of the stew. —*WHAT MRS. FISHER KNOWS ABOUT OLD SOUTHERN COOKING*, 1881

ORIGINAL RECIPE BLOOPER: Mrs. Fisher had been a slave and had never been taught to read. She dictated her recipes to transcribers, who misheard "succotash" and wrote "circuit hash" instead. The transcribers also misheard Mrs. Fisher's pronunciation of "crullers," in another recipe, and wrote "carolas."

*Frankly, my dear, I don't give a damn!* —CLARK GABLE, *GONE WITH THE WIND*, 1939

*Gone with the Wind,* filmed in the 1930s but set during the Civil War, has its share of bloopers. A 1930s sedan can be spotted driving by the veranda, a desk lamp has an electric cord, and a street lamppost has an electric lightbulb. Forty-eight states are mentioned early in the movie, but during the Civil War there were only thirty-four. There weren't forty-eight states in America until the 1930s, when the movie was made.

# CORN FRITTERS

*You think I'm an ignorant savage. . . . But still I cannot see if the savage one is me.*

*How can there be so much that you don't know?*

VOICE OF JUDY KUHN, *POCAHONTAS*, 1995

☆  ☆  ☆

Native Americans taught the early settlers how to grow corn. Some varieties of corn were raised for eating fresh, while others were for drying to make hominy or pone, both Indian words. Corn was always planted with climbing beans, which not only provided a complete protein when eaten with the corn, but also enriched the soil.

| | |
|---|---|
| 1½ CUPS CORN KERNELS | 1 TABLESPOON ALL-PURPOSE FLOUR |
| 3 LARGE EGGS | SALT AND PEPPER |
| 2 TABLESPOONS HEAVY CREAM | PEANUT OR VEGETABLE OIL |
| ½ CUP CORNFLAKE CRUMBS | |

1. Put ¾ cup of the corn kernels into a food processor and puree it. Stir in the remaining ¾ cup kernels. Reserve.

2. In a large bowl, whisk together the eggs and heavy cream. Stir in the cornflake crumbs and flour until combined. Add the corn, season with salt and pepper, and mix until incorporated.

3. Pour peanut oil into a small, heavy-bottomed pot to a depth of about 1 inch and heat over medium-high heat. Drop teaspoonfuls of the corn mixture, 2 or 3 at a time, into the oil and fry until golden, turning once. Transfer to a paper-towel-lined plate and sprinkle with salt. Serve warm.

---

*—What the hell's this?*

*—That's a low-cholesterol meal. Happy Valentine's.*

*—God! Are you trying to kill me?*

*—If I was gonna kill you, I'd use my hands.*

—GAILARD SARTAIN AND KATHY BATES, *FRIED GREEN TOMATOES*, 1991

Pemmican, made from pounded dried meat mixed with clarified fat and dried berries, was a long-lasting healthful food eaten between hunts or during travel. It contained all the essential nutrients and, thanks to the wild berries always included in the recipe, prevented scurvy.

---

# BUTTERMILK BISCUITS

SERVES 8

☆  ☆  ☆

This recipe comes from *The Virginia House-wife*, America's first regional cookbook (written by Mary Randolph in 1824) and considered by many as one of our nation's finest culinary works. These flaky, moist biscuits are perfect with the fried chicken on page 74.

2 CUPS ALL-PURPOSE FLOUR

2 TEASPOONS SUGAR

1 TEASPOON BAKING POWDER

1 TEASPOON SALT

½ TEASPOON BAKING SODA

6 TABLESPOONS (¾ STICK) COLD UNSALTED BUTTER, CUT INTO SMALL PIECES

¾ CUP BUTTERMILK

1. Preheat the oven to 400 degrees. Line a baking sheet with parchment paper and set aside.

2. In a large bowl, stir together the flour, sugar, baking powder, salt, and baking soda until well combined. Work in the butter with a fork and then add the buttermilk. Stir until the dough comes together.

3. Gently knead the dough in the bowl for 1 minute and then pat it out on a floured work surface to about ½ inch thick. Using a 2½-inch round cutter, cut 8 biscuits out of the dough. Transfer to the baking sheet and bake for about 12 minutes, or until golden.

---

*Oh, well, I guess some like it hot. I personally prefer classical music.* —TONY CURTIS, *SOME LIKE IT HOT*, 1959

The oven thermometer was invented in England in the 1850s but did not become commonly available until the 1900s. In America's early years, cookbook authors used terms like "bake in a slow oven," meaning at medium heat, or "bake quickly," when the oven needed to be very hot.

# PEANUT "COFFEE"

SERVES 4

*No more caffeine for you!*

VOICE OF DAVEIGH CHASE, *LILO AND STITCH*, 2002

☆   ☆   ☆

During the Civil War, to replace hard-to-come-by and expensive coffee, a hot beverage was made from roasted and ground peanuts. This deliciously creamy dairy-free drink, great hot or cold, comes from an 1885 recipe. For variety, try it with cashew butter instead.

½ CUP CREAMY PEANUT BUTTER

2 TABLESPOONS SUGAR

¼ TEASPOON GROUND CINNAMON

DASH OF VANILLA EXTRACT

CAYENNE PEPPER

Puree the peanut butter, sugar, cinnamon, and vanilla extract with 3 cups of cold water in a blender until smooth. Serve cold, or heat in a small saucepan, garnished with a sprinkle of cayenne.

---

*I don't care what you say about the soup, but don't pick on the coffee; it's too weak to fight back.*

—GINGER ROGERS, *THE PRIMROSE PATH*, 1940

A strong cup of black coffee always accompanied dessert down south. The birthplace of coffee is Africa, where it was originally eaten, not drunk. The ripe wild coffee beans were crushed in stone mortars and combined with other ingredients to form a nutritious snack. Raw coffee, rich in protein, loses its nutritional value when it is roasted.

# SUGAR CRISPS WITH CHOCOLATE DIPPING SAUCE

SERVES 12

*You finally guessed my favorite . . . hot chocolate!*

JOHNNY DEPP, *CHOCOLAT*, 2000

☆   ☆   ☆

These cookies were called "chocolate cakes" in the original 1824 recipe but were made without even a hint of chocolate or cocoa. I was intrigued by the missing ingredient mentioned in the name of the cookies, so I did a little research and discovered that in those days chocolate was only drunk as the beverage hot chocolate and not yet used in baking. These yummy "chocolate cakes" got their name because they were for dipping into hot chocolate. In this modern version, I create a thick dipping sauce based on hot chocolate recipes of the time.

4 TABLESPOONS (½ STICK) UNSALTED BUTTER, SOFTENED

½ CUP PACKED DARK BROWN SUGAR

¼ CUP MILK, AT ROOM TEMPERATURE

1¼ CUPS ALL-PURPOSE FLOUR, PLUS MORE AS NEEDED

COARSE SUGAR, SUCH AS TURBINADO

¾ CUP HEAVY CREAM

2 TEASPOONS LIGHT CORN SYRUP

3 TABLESPOONS UNSWEETENED COCOA POWDER

¼ CUP CONFECTIONERS' SUGAR

1. In a bowl, using an electric mixer, cream the butter and brown sugar together until fluffy. Add the milk and mix at medium speed until smooth. Stir in the flour until combined. Wrap the dough tightly in plastic wrap and flatten it into a disk. Refrigerate for at least 30 minutes.

2. Preheat the oven to 375 degrees. Line a baking sheet with parchment paper and set aside.

3. Lightly flour a work surface. Roll the dough out to about ⅛ inch thick. Cut the dough into strips 1 inch wide by 6 inches long. Transfer the strips to the lined baking sheet. Sprinkle the strips with coarse sugar and bake for 7 to 8 minutes, until golden. Allow to cool before serving.

4. While the crisps are baking, make the dipping sauce. In a small saucepan, heat the cream and corn syrup over medium-low heat until just simmering. Whisk in the cocoa powder and confectioners' sugar until well combined.

5. Serve the crisps with the warm sauce on the side.

*Are you hinting that my apples aren't what they ought to be?*

—ABE DINOVITCH, AS A TREE, *THE WIZARD OF OZ*, 1939

American as apple pie? Well, not quite. Apple pie is actually English. America's first apple pie recipes were from England, brought over in English cookbooks by English settlers. Apples are not even indigenous to the Americas. Saplings and apple seeds were brought over by English colonists, too.

# BOURBON SWEET POTATO PIE

SERVES 8

*I have come to the conclusion that one useless man is called a disgrace, that two are called a law firm, and that three or more become a Congress!*

WILLIAM DANIELS, *1776*, 1972

☆　☆　☆

In America's early years, sugar was sold as hard-packed cones wrapped in blue paper, which had to be scraped loose or cut into small chunks with special sugar nips.

This outstanding sweet potato pie delicately flavored with bourbon is a southern favorite. Try it with a scoop of ice cream or topped with whipped cream mixed with bourbon and maple syrup.

> 2 LARGE SWEET POTATOES, PEELED AND BOILED
>
> 4 TABLESPOONS (½ STICK) UNSALTED BUTTER, SOFTENED
>
> ¾ CUP PACKED DARK BROWN SUGAR, PLUS MORE FOR GARNISH
>
> 2 OUNCES BOURBON
>
> ¼ TEASPOON GROUND NUTMEG
>
> GRATED ZEST OF 2 LEMONS
>
> 4 LARGE EGGS
>
> 1 READY-MADE 9-INCH DEEP-DISH PIECRUST

1. Preheat the oven to 375 degrees.

2. Mash the sweet potatoes, while they are still warm, in a large bowl. Add the butter, brown sugar, bourbon, nutmeg, and zest of 1 of the lemons and stir until well combined.

3. In a separate bowl, beat the eggs. Add the eggs to the sweet potato mixture and stir well to combine. Pour the mixture into the piecrust and bake for 35 to 40 minutes, until the filling is firm and the crust golden.

4. Allow to cool on a rack. When cool, top with a sprinkle of brown sugar and the zest of the remaining lemon.

**ORIGINAL RECIPE: SWEET POTATO PUDDING**—Boil one pound of sweet potatos [*sic*] very tender, rub them while hot through a colander, add six eggs, well beaten, three quarters of a pound of powdered sugar, three quarters of butter, and some grated nutmeg and lemon-peel, with a glass of brandy; put a paste in the dish, and when the pudding is done, sprinkle the top with sugar, and cover it with bits of citron. Irish potato pudding made in the same manner, but is not so good. —*THE VIRGINIA HOUSE-WIFE,* 1824

# SOUTHERN PEACH ICE CREAM

SERVES 6

*—May I sit here?*

*—It's a free country—or at least, it will be.*

AN UNCREDITED ACTOR AND MEL GIBSON, *THE PATRIOT,* 2000

☆  ☆  ☆

During the summer of 1790, while in New York City, George Washington reportedly spent the then extraordinary sum of $200 for ice cream. Thomas Jefferson, Alexander Hamilton, and Dolley Madison were just a few of the other early Americans who made ice cream, the creamy Italian introduction to our shores, an American staple.

½ CUP SUGAR

2 CUPS SLICED PEELED PEACHES (ABOUT 1 POUND)

2 TEASPOONS FRESHLY SQUEEZED LEMON JUICE

1 CUP HEAVY CREAM

1.  In a large bowl, sprinkle the sugar over the peaches. Stir gently and set aside for 30 minutes. In a blender or food processor, puree the sugared peaches and any juices they expelled until very smooth. Stir in the lemon juice and cream until well combined.

2.  Freeze the peach mixture in an ice-cream machine according to the manufacturer's instructions.

---

*—You do know Elvis is dead, right?*

*—No, Elvis is not dead. He just went home.*

—WILL SMITH AND TOMMY LEE JONES, *MEN IN BLACK,* 1997

*Love Me Tender,* a Civil War story, is the only movie Elvis ever made where he did not get top billing. The Yankee uniforms are shown in the film as having zippers, a movie blooper. Zippers hadn't been invented yet and were not used on military clothing until World War I.

# ALL-AMERICAN PICNIC

Fourth of July weekend—a perfect time of year for an old-fashioned picnic—is also a perfect time for eating fresh-picked corn. I spend the Fourth of July in the Berkshires, which still keep some old-fashioned customs, such as selling corn roadside on the honor system. Over twenty years ago, on my first visit to the Berkshires, jaded New Yorker that I was, I predicted that the corn, the money box, and the chalk signboard we were passing on the way to Tanglewood would be stolen. What a pleasant surprise to notice on the drive back from the concert that not only was the bushel empty and the money box full, but satisfied customers had even written thank-you notes on the chalkboard! I've been hooked on the Berkshires ever since.

It wouldn't be the Fourth of July without red, white, and blue, of course, so I decorate the picnic table with a dark blue cloth and add bright red napkins tied with white daisy chains. I set out a large clear-glass bowl of hard-boiled eggs in a mix of colors, some left natural white and others dyed red or blue. Kids love to color eggs, so why do it only at Easter? Colored eggs are a great decoration and a terrific picnic food. Serve them with small bowls of red horseradish mixed with mayonnaise.

For drinks, in honor of the Boston Tea Party, I serve pitchers of iced tea with red ice cubes made from raspberry or Red Zinger tea. I also fill a wheelbarrow with ice and assorted beers and soft drinks. Of course, no summer picnic would be complete without mint juleps. I follow the 1700s advice to make it by the glass. I set out the ingredients and directions from the original recipe and let everyone fix their own. I like mine minty and sweet, so I bruise about 6 mint leaves in a tall glass and shake with 2 tablespoons of superfine sugar and lots of crushed ice. Once the sugar is dissolved, I add a shot or two of bourbon.

My kids enjoy the Fourth and always devise activities for the younger guests. One favorite is "pin the star on the flag." All the kids paint the flag's stripes on an old sheet and cut stars out of paper plates. Once the paint dries, the stars get backed with double-stick tape. Then everyone, adults included, is blindfolded and spun around. The stars can end up in some pretty odd places, especially after several mint juleps! We usually declare two winners, one for closest to the flag and one for most creative miss.

In keeping with our family's tradition of recycling favorite holiday activities (like coloring eggs in July), we build a gingerbread house and decorate it like a log cabin or the White House, depending on what candy architectural features we like that year.

Our picnic usually ends with a verse or two of "Yankee Doodle Dandy," the song made popular during the Revolutionary War. Then, when it's too mosquito-y and dark to stay outdoors, we come in and watch James Cagney sing it while we have dessert. I like edible decorations, so the dessert table usually includes bowls of strawberries, blueberries, and whipped cream, along with the other sweets.

## Movie Suggestions

### PRE-REVOLUTION

*Amistad,* 1997. Africans aboard a slave ship escape and seek freedom in 1839 America. Directed by
   Steven Spielberg; stars Anthony Hopkins and Morgan Freeman.

*Apache,* 1954. Burt Lancaster stars as an Indian in Geronimo's standoff with the cavalry.

*Band of Angels,* 1957. Clark Gable, Yvonne De Carlo, and Sidney Poitier star in the story of a mixed-
   blood orphan sold as a slave.

*Black Robe,* 1991. Australian film about Native Americans, set in 1634.

*Christopher Columbus: The Discovery,* 1992. Tale of Columbus's voyage, starring Tom Selleck, Marlon Brando, and Catherine Zeta-Jones.

*Roots,* 1977. Miniseries about one African-American family's experience, told over several generations. Stars Ben Vereen, Cicely Tyson, and Leslie Uggams.

## THE REVOLUTION

*The Howards of Virginia,* 1940. Cary Grant plays a backwoodsman who marries a rich Virginia woman.

*John Paul Jones,* 1959. Story of "I have not yet begun to fight" hero, John Paul Jones, played by Robert Stack.

*Johnny Tremain and the Sons of Liberty,* 1957. Movie about the Boston Tea Party, starring Sebastian Cabot.

*The Patriot,* 2000. Epic starring Mel Gibson and Heath Ledger.

*Revolution,* 1985. Story of our fight for independence from England. Stars Al Pacino and Donald Sutherland.

*1776,* 1972. Musical comedy about the signing of the Constitution, starring Blythe Danner.

*The Time of Their Lives,* 1946. Abbott and Costello comedy about a pair of Revolutionary War ghosts who haunt a modern mansion.

## THE CIVIL WAR YEARS

*Abe Lincoln in Illinois,* 1940. Raymond Massey plays Lincoln in this superb movie (my son, Max, wants to know why history class can't be as interesting) written by Robert Sherwood, based on his Pulitzer Prize–winning play.

*The Adventures of Mark Twain,* 1944. Story of Mark Twain's trip along the Mississippi and on to California for the Gold Rush.

*Bad Company,* 1972. Two Civil War draft dodgers roam the West. Stars Jeff Bridges.

*The Beguiled,* 1971. Clint Eastwood plays a wounded Union soldier taken in by a southern all-girls' school.

*The Blue and the Gray,* 1982. Miniseries starring Gregory Peck and Lloyd Bridges.

*Cavalry Charge,* 1962. Ronald Reagan action adventure.

*Copper Canyon,* 1950. Hedy Lamarr and Ray Milland star in a post–Civil War romance.

*Dark Command,* 1940. John Wayne and Roy Rogers in the story of outlaws in Kansas during the Civil War.

*Friendly Persuasion,* 1956. A Quaker family's conflicts during the Civil War, starring Gary Cooper and Anthony Perkins.

*The General,* 1927. Buster Keaton Civil War silent classic, remade in 1956 as *The Great Locomotive Chase.*

*Gettysburg,* 1993. Based on the Pulitzer Prize–winning Civil War novel, this is the only movie ever to be filmed on the Gettysburg National Park Battlefield.

*Glory,* 1989. Matthew Broderick, Denzel Washington, and Morgan Freeman star in the story of the first all-black volunteer army unit.

*Gone with the Wind,* 1939. Classic starring Vivien Leigh and Clark Gable.

*Love Me Tender,* 1956. Elvis Presley sings the title song in this saga of a Civil War–torn family.

*The Red Badge of Courage,* 1951. Based on Stephen Crane's novel about the conflict between the North and South.

*Shenandoah,* 1965. James Stewart stars as a Virginia farmer struggling during the Civil War.

*Young Mr. Lincoln,* 1939. Must-see biography of Lincoln's early years. Stars Henry Fonda.

# THE WILD WEST

## COMING ATTRACTIONS
TEXAS CHILI ★ NATIVE AMERICAN FRY BREAD

## FEATURE PRESENTATION
BARBECUE CHICKEN ★ PAN-SEARED STEAK AND ONIONS
GRILLED RIVER CATCH WITH PIQUANT RELISH ★ OLD WEST BAKED BEANS
TEXAS YELLOW "COLD SLAW" ★ TWICE-BAKED ONION POTATOES

## CLOSING CREDITS
SKILLET BROWN BETTY ★ CHUCK WAGON MOLASSES-COFFEE CHEWS ★ STOVE-TOP CHERRY PIE

## LIGHTS, CAMERA, ACTION! RANCH HOUSE ROUNDUP SUPPER
MOVIE SUGGESTIONS

*Five generations, a mere 120 years ago, this land was known only as
the West. The West that was won by its pioneers, settlers, and adventurers
is long gone now, yet it is theirs forever, for they left tracks in history that will
never be eroded by wind or rain, never plowed under by tractors.*

—SPENCER TRACY, *HOW THE WEST WAS WON*, 1962

Cattle drives, cowboys, saloon brawls, six-shooters, outlaws, stagecoach and train robberies, and riding off into the sunset with (but most likely without) the girl make for great stories. There are hundreds of terrific Westerns that were created by Hollywood (even in Japan and Italy!), such as *Dances with Wolves, Unforgiven, High Noon,* and *The Good, the Bad, and the Ugly,* featuring stars we've come to associate with the West, such as Kevin Costner, Clint Eastwood, John Wayne, and Gene Hackman.

During its Wild West days, the 1800s, America was on the move and eating on the run. By midcentury, almost a half-million settlers had gone out west seeking homesteads. From surviving diaries and purchase documents, we know more or less exactly what provisions these settlers packed in their covered wagons. One family of four made it across the continent on 824 pounds of flour, 725 pounds of salt pork, 200 pounds of lard, 200 pounds of dried beans, 160 pounds of molasses and brown sugar, 135 pounds of dried peaches and apples, 75 pounds of coffee, 25 pounds of salt, and some pepper and baking soda. This was fairly typical for most, with the exception of the forty-niners, or gold rushers, who always included at least one keg of whiskey on their list.

Chuck wagon cooks had to be mighty creative to turn the limited ingredients in a typical chuck box into months of tasty meals. Cooks on the range, affectionately called "Miss Sally" or "Cookie," were highly respected and well paid, often receiving twice the salary of a cowboy. A good cook was, after all, essential to keeping hungry cowpokes satisfied and a drive running smoothly.

So, just what did cowboys eat on roundups? What did those chuck wagon cooks prepare out on the prairie?

As you can probably guess, dried beans and cured pork—used to make the camp-side staple pork and beans—were a part of every meal. Another staple, flour, was used for sourdough biscuits, flapjacks, and pan dumplings, and was even boiled with water and molasses for a hearty after-dinner sweet pudding. Game—snared or shot—provided fresh meat and variety to the menu, as did fresh produce purchased along the trail.

For holidays, the "cookie" would prepare a special meal. Wrote camp cook Oliver Nelson in 1880, "For Christmas that year I sent to Caldwell for some extras—lemon flavorings and such. I roasted two turkeys, which the boys sent up from the south camp, and I baked two cakes sixteen inches across and four inches high—baked them in the Dutch ovens."

Dishes were given colorful names such as "Son of a Bitch," a stew of tough meats simmered tender and tasty; "Moonshine," white rice slow-cooked with sweet raisins; "Cow Bosom," sourdough bread that didn't rise; "Cracklin'," corn bread flavored with crisp pork skins; and "Plum Duff," a wild plum and flour pudding served with fried panfish.

The following recipes come from cowboys' diaries and various cookbooks of the 1800s and provide a sample of the varied and delicious foods of the West. So, as they said back then, tie on the feed bag and set a spell.

# TEXAS CHILI

*Of course he had a gun. This is Texas!*
*Everybody has a gun. My florist has a gun!*

CANDICE BERGEN, *MISS CONGENIALITY*, 2000

☆ ☆ ☆

Chili con carne, meat with chili peppers, was probably first developed on the Texas-Mexico border somewhere near San Antonio in the early 1800s. There is endless debate about what constitutes authentic chili and whether it should contain beans or not. I've opted for a beanless Lone Star version, which Texans call "a bowl of red," and modernized it by using a jar of my favorite salsa instead of the usual tomato paste.

4 OUNCES BACON, DICED

1 LARGE RED ONION, DICED

3 GARLIC CLOVES, MINCED

2 POUNDS ROUND STEAK, CUT INTO ½-INCH
    CUBES

4 CUPS BEEF STOCK

ONE 16-OUNCE JAR TOMATO SALSA

ONE 8-OUNCE JAR GREEN CHOPPED CHILIES,
    DRAINED

2 TEASPOONS CHILI POWDER

½ TEASPOON DRIED OREGANO

½ TEASPOON GROUND CUMIN

3 TABLESPOONS FINELY GROUND CORNMEAL

SALT AND PEPPER

RED PEPPER FLAKES, CAYENNE PEPPER, OR
    CHIPOTLE POWDER (OPTIONAL)

1. In a large, heavy-bottomed pot, cook the bacon over medium-high heat until the fat is rendered, about 4 minutes. Add the onion and cook until golden, about 8 minutes. Stir in the garlic and cook until softened, 2 to 3 minutes. Add the steak and cook, turning frequently, until browned, about 5 minutes.

2. Stir in the beef stock, salsa, chilies, chili powder, oregano, and cumin and bring to a boil. Reduce the heat to maintain a simmer and cook, uncovered, until the steak is tender, about 45 minutes.

3. Carefully remove about ½ cup of the liquid and stir the cornmeal into the liquid until smooth. Pour the mixture back into the pot and simmer until thickened, about 10 minutes. Season with salt and pepper and add red pepper flakes, cayenne, or chipotle powder to taste.

# NATIVE AMERICAN FRY BREAD

SERVES 6

*As I heard my Sioux name being called over and over,*
*I knew for the first time who I really was.*

KEVIN COSTNER, *DANCES WITH WOLVES*, 1990

☆　☆　☆

My mother was taught how to make fry bread while visiting Arapaho relatives on a Cheyenne reservation in Wyoming. Besides this wonderful recipe, she came home with a "talking stick," used at tribal meetings to indicate who has the floor, and a "dream catcher," a hoop with crisscrossed gut string, beads, and feathers hung by the bed to catch nightmares.

Easy to prepare, this chewy griddle bread has been made the same way for hundreds of years.

| | |
|---|---|
| 3 CUPS ALL-PURPOSE FLOUR, PLUS MORE AS NEEDED | 1 TEASPOON SALT |
| | 1¼ CUPS MILK |
| 1 TABLESPOON BAKING POWDER | VEGETABLE OIL |

1. In a large bowl, stir together the flour, baking powder, and salt until combined. Add the milk and stir with a wooden spoon until a dough forms. Knead the dough for about 2 minutes, or until smooth and elastic, adding more flour if necessary. Wrap the dough in plastic wrap and allow to rest for 20 minutes.

2. Divide the dough into 12 equal-sized balls. Using your hands, press the dough balls flat to a thickness of about ¼ inch. Poke a large hole in each with your finger. (They will look like doughnuts.)

3. Pour vegetable oil into a nonstick frying pan to a depth of about ⅛ inch and heat over medium heat. Fry the bread rounds, turning once, until golden and puffy, about 1 minute per side. Transfer to a paper-towel-lined plate to drain. Serve warm.

---

*—You wish to see the frontier?*
*—Yes, sir, before it's gone.*

—MAURY CHAYKIN AND KEVIN COSTNER, *DANCES WITH WOLVES*, 1990

*Dances with Wolves* was the first Western in sixty years to win Best Picture, following *Cimarron,* which won in 1931. Kevin Costner, the film's star and director, used authentic Sioux-Lakota language in the movie's dialogue and received praise from the Native American community for his portrayal of their culture.

# BARBECUE CHICKEN

SERVES 4

*Between two evils, I always pick the one I haven't tried before.*

MAE WEST, *GO WEST YOUNG MAN*, 1936

☆ ☆ ☆

"Barbecue," originally the name for the wooden frame used by Native Americans to dry meat over open fires, later came to mean a big community cookout.

This finger-licking sauce, perfect for chicken and also wonderful with burgers, fish, or steak, is a combination of two sauces from an 1867 cookbook. One was a spicy mustard marinade and the other a tomato-based barbecue sauce.

½ CUP KETCHUP

2 TABLESPOONS HONEY MUSTARD

1 TABLESPOON CIDER VINEGAR

2 TEASPOONS TOMATO PASTE

1 TEASPOON WORCESTERSHIRE SAUCE

1 TEASPOON SALT

¼ TEASPOON CAYENNE PEPPER

¼ TEASPOON CHILI POWDER

¼ TEASPOON BLACK PEPPER

¼ TEASPOON CURRY POWDER

¼ TEASPOON GARLIC POWDER

3 TABLESPOONS VEGETABLE OIL

1 CHICKEN (ABOUT 4 POUNDS), CUT INTO
SERVING PIECES

1. In a bowl, whisk together the ketchup, mustard, vinegar, tomato paste, Worcestershire sauce, salt, cayenne, chili powder, black pepper, curry powder, and garlic powder until well combined. Slowly whisk in the vegetable oil in a slow, steady stream until smooth. Reserve ¼ cup of the sauce in a small bowl to serve with the cooked chicken.

2. Coat the chicken with the remaining sauce and allow the chicken to marinate, covered, in the refrigerator for at least 1 hour.

3. Preheat an outdoor gas grill to medium-high heat or prepare a medium-hot fire in a charcoal grill.

4. When the grill is hot, reduce the gas grill to medium, or pile the charcoal to one side of the charcoal grill. Grill the chicken, turning frequently, until the juices run clear when it is pierced with a fork, about 35 minutes.

5. Serve with the reserved ¼ cup barbecue sauce.

*There's always a man faster on the draw than you are, and the more you use a gun, the sooner you're gonna run into that man.*

—BURT LANCASTER,
*GUNFIGHT AT THE O.K. CORRAL*, 1957

William Bonney, the legendary outlaw nicknamed Billy the Kid born in 1859, inspired dozens of movies, including *Billy the Kid, I Shot Billy the Kid, Oath of Vengeance, Texas Trouble Shooters, Trigger Men,* and *The Young Guns.* Wild Bill Hickok and Wyatt Earp, legendary good guys, were also favorite Hollywood characters, each featured in movies such as *Gunfight at the O.K. Corral, Pony Express, Little Big Man,* and *Tombstone.*

# PAN-SEARED STEAK AND ONIONS

SERVES 4

*Hey, mister, will you stake a fellow American to a meal?*

HUMPHREY BOGART, *THE TREASURE OF THE SIERRA MADRE*, 1948

☆  ☆  ☆

Usually cooked over an open fire in an iron skillet, this stove-top-seared steak with bourbon-flavored onions is excellent eaten with sourdough bread. Sourdough, developed during the gold rush years, was made with a yeast starter of flour mixed with water until it fermented and soured.

4 TABLESPOONS (½ STICK) BUTTER

2 TABLESPOONS OLIVE OIL

2 LARGE ONIONS, SLICED

1 BONELESS SIRLOIN STEAK (ABOUT 2 POUNDS)

SALT AND PEPPER

½ CUP BOURBON

1. In a large skillet, melt 2 tablespoons of the butter with 1 tablespoon of the olive oil over medium heat. Add the onions and cook, stirring occasionally, until golden, about 15 minutes. Transfer the onions to a bowl and set aside.

2. Generously season both sides of the steak with salt and pepper. Add the remaining 1 tablespoon of the oil to the skillet and fry the steak over medium heat, turning once, until browned, about 6 minutes per side for medium. Transfer the steak to a serving platter and cover to keep warm.

3. Add the bourbon to the skillet and, over medium heat, scrape up any bits that cling to the pan. Allow the liquor to simmer until reduced by half, about 1 minute. Add the onions and the remaining 2 tablespoons butter and stir until the butter is melted. Reduce the heat and gently simmer until the onions are heated through, about 2 minutes. Season to taste with salt and pepper and stir in any juices that have run off from the steak.

4. To serve, cut the steak into ¼-inch-thick slices and top with the onions.

> *. . . Shoot first, shoot later, shoot some more, and then when everybody's dead, try to ask a question or two.*
>
> —KEVIN KLINE, *WILD WILD WEST*, 1999
>
> Test audiences were so confused by the initial version of *Wild Wild West*—a movie about two nineteenth-century hired guns fighting an evil inventor—that at first they weren't sure if it was a comedy or not. The producers added additional humorous dialogue to clear things up.

# GRILLED RIVER CATCH WITH PIQUANT RELISH

SERVES 4

*Next time you fellows strike it rich, holler for me, will you, before you start splashing water around? Water's precious. Sometimes, it can be more precious than gold.*

WALTER HUSTON, *THE TREASURE OF THE SIERRA MADRE*, 1948

☆ ☆ ☆

This recipe for grilled fish with a wonderfully spicy relish comes from an 1867 cookbook, which also contains instructions for the western favorites beef jerky and "camp stew," made with squirrel. To keep the campsite neat, chuck wagon cooks insisted that the cowboys scrape any leftovers into what they called "squirrel cans," big, empty lard tins. When a cowboy wanted to insult the grub, he would say that it tasted like it was "dipped out of the squirrel can."

With this moist and tasty fish on the menu, there won't be any complaints from your crew or any leftovers for the squirrel can.

1 PLUM TOMATO, CORED, SEEDED, AND FINELY
   CHOPPED
2 TABLESPOONS SWEET RELISH
1 TABLESPOON MAYONNAISE
JUICE OF ½ LEMON OR LIME
½ TEASPOON BOTTLED HORSERADISH

2 DASHES OF TABASCO SAUCE
SALT AND PEPPER
4 SMALL TROUT (ABOUT 14 OUNCES EACH),
   CLEANED
OLIVE OIL

1. To prepare the piquant relish, stir together the tomato, sweet relish, mayonnaise, lemon juice, horseradish, and Tabasco sauce in a small bowl until combined. Season to taste with salt and pepper. Cover with plastic wrap and refrigerate until ready to serve.

2. Meanwhile, preheat an outdoor gas grill to medium-high heat, or prepare a medium-hot fire in a charcoal grill.

3. Rinse the trout thoroughly under cold running water and pat dry with paper towels. Lightly rub each trout with olive oil and season inside and out with salt and pepper. Grill the trout until opaque through the center, about 4 minutes per side.

4. Serve the grilled trout with the piquant relish on the side.

---

*We cut down my percentage . . . liable to interfere with my aim.*

—CLINT EASTWOOD, *THE GOOD, THE BAD, AND THE UGLY*, 1966

Clint Eastwood has starred in dozens of movies, including the first spaghetti Westerns, low-budget films made in Italy.

In 1993, he won Oscars for Best Picture and Best Director for his Western *Unforgiven*, about a wronged dance hall prostitute.

# OLD WEST BAKED BEANS

SERVES 8

☆　☆　☆

This slow-baked molasses-and-mustard-flavored western favorite is a perfect party food because it can be made days ahead and just gets better with time. Great served with the Native American Fry Bread on page 94.

Enjoy it while watching *Blazing Saddles,* which, according to creator Mel Brooks, is best seen on video. Claims Brooks, "I can't watch *Blazing Saddles* on television. . . . A lot of prudes got together and silly people got together and they cut out everything they thought would be offensive to a four-year-old."

1 POUND DRIED NAVY, PINTO, OR PINK BEANS

2 LARGE ONIONS, DICED

12 OUNCES SMOKED PORK OR HAM STEAK, CHOPPED

3 CUPS BEEF STOCK

$\frac{1}{4}$ TEASPOON CAYENNE PEPPER

$\frac{1}{4}$ CUP DARK MOLASSES

$\frac{1}{4}$ CUP KETCHUP

3 TABLESPOONS DARK BROWN SUGAR, PLUS MORE AS NEEDED

SALT AND PEPPER

1. Soak the beans overnight in water in a large bowl.

2. Preheat the oven to 375 degrees.

3. Sauté the onions and pork over medium heat in a large casserole until the onions are tender, about 10 minutes. Add the drained beans, beef stock, cayenne, molasses, ketchup, brown sugar, and salt and pepper to taste and bring to a boil.

4. Cover the casserole and transfer to the oven. Bake for $3\frac{1}{2}$ to 4 hours, until the beans are tender.

5. Serve topped with a sprinkle of brown sugar.

*Is that a ten-gallon hat, or are you just enjoying the show?* —MADELINE KAHN, *BLAZING SADDLES,* 1974

*Blazing Saddles* is the all-time highest-grossing Western ever made, described in promotional materials as "Mel Brooks' comic saga of cowboys and imbeciles."

Richard Pryor was originally considered for the role of the sheriff, but due to his controversial comedy routines, Brooks opted for Cleavon Little instead. The film caused controversy anyway. The movie was criticized for using the word "nigger," which Brooks defends, saying, "I don't think the word should be used, unless it's used absolutely correctly, . . . to show prejudice."

A second controversy occurred when the real Hedy Lamarr sued for the use of the name Hedley Lamarr in the film, and the third came when animal-rights activists protested the film's mistreatment of horses. According to Brooks, "I got over 1,000 letters from animal lovers who thought that I actually had Alex Karras as Mongo smash the horse in the face and knock it out. He missed it by a foot."

# TEXAS YELLOW "COLD SLAW"

SERVES 6

*I'm a Texas woman, which means I have no need*
*for a man to keep things running.*

RACHEL GRIFFITHS, *THE ROOKIE*, 2002

☆　☆　☆

The word "coleslaw" comes from the Dutch, but Texans renamed it "cold slaw" and branded it their own by preparing it without mayonnaise. Here, crunchy cabbage, cucumbers, and peppers are tossed with an onion-turmeric vinaigrette, which not only makes the onion sweet and mellow, but also gives the entire mix wonderful color. This must-try side dish is one of my favorite summer picnic salads, as it holds up unrefrigerated for hours and gets rave reviews.

| | |
|---|---|
| ¼ CUP CIDER VINEGAR | 1 SMALL ONION, FINELY DICED |
| 2 TABLESPOONS DARK BROWN SUGAR | ½ SMALL HEAD CABBAGE, COARSELY CHOPPED |
| ½ TEASPOON CELERY SEED | 1 CUCUMBER, PEELED, SEEDED, AND DICED |
| ½ TEASPOON GROUND TURMERIC | ½ GREEN BELL PEPPER, COARSELY CHOPPED |
| ¼ TEASPOON GROUND GINGER | 3 TABLESPOONS OLIVE OIL |
| PINCH OF GROUND ALLSPICE | SALT AND PEPPER |

1. In a small saucepan, bring the vinegar, brown sugar, celery seed, turmeric, ginger, and allspice to a boil over medium-high heat. Stir in the onion, remove from the heat, and allow to stand for 5 minutes to cool.

2. Meanwhile, toss the cabbage, cucumber, and bell pepper together in a serving bowl.

3. Whisk the olive oil into the cooled vinegar mixture until combined. Pour the onion-turmeric vinaigrette over the vegetables and toss to coat. Season to taste with salt and pepper and serve.

# TWICE-BAKED ONION POTATOES

SERVES 4

*I never heard of him [Shakespeare].*

*What part of Texas he from?*

ALAN HALE, *DODGE CITY*, 1939

☆   ☆   ☆

This 1876 recipe for onion-filled twice-baked potatoes was named "Texas Baked Irish Potatoes." Even though white potatoes were originally from the Americas—exported to Europe only after Columbus—they have nevertheless always been associated with Ireland. Besides baked, fried, and boiled, cowboys liked to eat potatoes raw after they'd been soaked overnight in salt and vinegar.

4 LARGE BAKING POTATOES

10 TABLESPOONS (1 STICK PLUS 2 TABLESPOONS) BUTTER

1 LARGE ONION, FINELY DICED

SALT AND PEPPER

1. Preheat the oven to 375 degrees.

2. Place the potatoes on a baking sheet and bake for 45 to 50 minutes, until potatoes are cooked through and can be easily pieced with a knife. Remove the potatoes from the oven and increase the oven temperature to 475 degrees.

3. When cool enough to handle, make a slit across the top of each potato without cutting all the way through. Gently push on the sides of the potato to loosen the meat, but do not tear the skins. With a large spoon, remove as much of the meat as possible and transfer it to a bowl. Place the empty skins on a lightly buttered baking sheet.

4. Add 8 tablespoons of the butter and the onion to the potato meat and mash. Season with salt and pepper to taste, put the potato mixture back into the skins, and dot each potato with the remaining 2 tablespoons butter. Bake about 20 minutes, until the tops brown. Serve hot.

---

*Never apologize, mister. It's a sign of weakness.* —JOHN WAYNE, *SHE WORE A YELLOW RIBBON,* 1949

My husband must have misheard this line as "Never ask directions, mister. It's a sign of weakness." How those trailblazers made it out west without me nagging them to stop for directions, I'll never understand.

# SKILLET BROWN BETTY

SERVES 6

*—What did you say your name was again?*

*—I didn't.*

BILLY CURTIS AND CLINT EASTWOOD, *HIGH PLAINS DRIFTER*, 1973

☆   ☆   ☆

Food historians aren't sure how this dessert got its name. A favorite since colonial times, brown Betty is surely of English origin, and I'm guessing that it comes from the abbreviation of the then-popular British name Elizabeth.

This modern version is quick to prepare, using graham crackers and dried apples. I like to add a splash of whiskey to the Betty and even serve it topped with whipped cream or ice cream mixed with a jolt more. For the little saddles, you can make a virgin Betty.

6 TABLESPOONS (¾ STICK) BUTTER

½ CUP PACKED DARK BROWN SUGAR

½ TEASPOON GROUND CINNAMON

2 CUPS APPLE JUICE OR WATER

JUICE OF 1 LEMON

10 OUNCES DRIED APPLE SLICES

2 TABLESPOONS WHISKEY (OPTIONAL)

1 CUP GRAHAM CRACKER CRUMBS (ABOUT 5 CRACKERS)

1. Preheat the oven to 500 degrees.

2. In a large ovenproof skillet, melt 4 tablespoons of the butter over medium heat. Add the brown sugar, cinnamon, and apple and lemon juices and bring to a boil. Add the apple slices and simmer, stirring frequently, until the liquid is nearly absorbed, about 15 minutes.

3. Remove from the heat. Stir in the whiskey, if using. Sprinkle the graham cracker crumbs evenly over the apples. Dot with the remaining 2 tablespoons butter and bake for about 5 minutes, until browned.

4. Serve warm, topped with your favorite ice cream or whipped cream.

---

*After a meal there's nothing like a good cigar.* —LEE VAN CLEEF, *THE GOOD, THE BAD, AND THE UGLY*, 1966

Native Americans introduced tobacco to early Spanish and Portuguese explorers, who brought it to Europe in the 1500s. Tobacco was first commercially cultivated in Virginia in the early 1600s, where it was used to make chewing and pipe tobacco as well as snuff. Cigars weren't invented until the 1800s.

# CHUCK WAGON MOLASSES-COFFEE CHEWS

MAKES ABOUT 2 DOZEN CHEWS

*—He did his share of killin'. . . .*

*—Yeah, only now he does his killin' with a coffee cup.*

WILLIAM HOLDEN AND ERNEST BORGNINE, *THE WILD BUNCH*, 1969

☆  ☆  ☆

This exchange about the perils of campfire coffee is from *The Wild Bunch*, directed by Sam Peckinpah. Many of the film's most famous scenes, such as the long walk by the Bunch and the train robbery, were not originally written into the script but improvised on the set.

These creamy, rich coffee chews make a classic ending to any meal.

1 CUP PACKED LIGHT BROWN SUGAR

½ CUP GRANULATED SUGAR

¼ CUP LIGHT CORN SYRUP

½ CUP STRONG BREWED COFFEE

¼ CUP EVAPORATED MILK

1 TABLESPOON BUTTER

1 TABLESPOON LIGHT OR DARK MOLASSES

1 TABLESPOON INSTANT COFFEE GRANULES

½ CUP CHOPPED PECANS

1. In a large, heavy-bottomed saucepan, stir together the brown sugar, granulated sugar, and corn syrup until combined. Put the pan over medium heat, add the brewed coffee and evaporated milk, and bring to a boil, stirring constantly. Reduce the heat to maintain a simmer, and cook, stirring frequently, until a candy thermometer inserted in the mixture reads 235 degrees or a small amount dropped into ice water forms a firm ball, about 20 minutes.

2. Remove from the heat and stir in the butter, molasses, coffee granules, and pecans until combined.

3. Using 2 greased teaspoons, quickly drop teaspoonfuls onto parchment or waxed paper and allow to cool completely.

# STOVE-TOP CHERRY PIE

SERVES 8

*We can't afford good wine or pink champagne,*
*We ain't got no open fireplace flame.*

BETTY BUCKLEY, *TENDER MERCIES*, 1983

☆　☆　☆

Betty Buckley, Tony Award–winning singer and actress, hails from the Lone Star State and descends from true western frontier stock. Her grandfather, "Kid" Buckley, was a real-life cowboy and her grandmother was a homesteader who cooked on cattle ranches throughout South Dakota back when it was still only a territory. Buckley clearly inherited her grandparents' rugged spirit, as she regularly competes in cutting-horse competitions on her quarter horse, Purple Badger.

I was inspired to create this modern stove-top recipe after hearing Betty rave about "Mom Buckley's" scrumptious sugar-topped cherry pie. Although Buckley's grandmother was known for her thin homemade crust, I've substituted the no-bake store-bought kind for us tinhorns.

TWO 12-OUNCE BAGS FROZEN PITTED CHERRIES, THAWED

½ CUP DRIED CHERRIES

1 CUP GRANULATED SUGAR

3 TABLESPOONS CORNSTARCH

2 TABLESPOONS UNSALTED BUTTER

1 TABLESPOON FRESHLY SQUEEZED LEMON JUICE

½ TEASPOON VANILLA EXTRACT

1 READY-MADE 9-INCH SHORTBREAD OR GRAHAM CRACKER CRUST

WHIPPED CREAM

LIGHT BROWN SUGAR

1. Put the thawed cherries, dried cherries, and granulated sugar in a saucepan and simmer over medium heat. Cook until the cherries begin to break down, about 20 minutes. Carefully remove about ½ cup of the liquid from the pan and allow to cool to room temperature. Stir in the cornstarch until smooth and add back to the simmering cherries. Cook, stirring, until the mixture thickens, about 2 minutes. Remove from the heat and add the butter, lemon juice, and vanilla extract and stir until the butter is melted. Pour into the crust and allow to cool to room temperature. Refrigerate for 2 hours, or until set.

2. Serve with a dollop of whipped cream topped with a sprinkling of brown sugar.

*—Give me your cup.*

*—I don't drink coffee, thank you.*

*—Well, now, what do you drink?*

*—I'm partial to cold buttermilk.*

—KIM DARBY AND JOHN WAYNE, *TRUE GRIT,* 1969

John Wayne starred in his first feature film, *The Big Trail,* in 1930, and after nearly 150 movies, finally received an Oscar in 1970 for his role as a one-eyed lawman in *True Grit.* At the Academy Awards ceremony, Wayne good-naturedly joked, "If I'd have known this was all it would take, I'd have put that eye patch on forty years ago."

# RANCH HOUSE ROUNDUP SUPPER

A roundup supper, fantastic outdoors during the warm summer months, is also a terrific way to cheer up a gloomy winter evening.

There are lots of props that can be used to create a Wild West feel, such as old cowboy boots or a ten-gallon hat filled with large Mexican paper flowers; horseshoes; checkerboards; and cactus plants. Colorful saddle blankets can double as tablecloths, old bandanas as napkins, and cast-iron skillets as candleholders.

Tin dishes or sturdy, compartmented plastic plates add a campsite feel. Serve the food buffet-style in huge pots and iron skillets and fill squirt bottles with ketchup or barbecue sauce so the kids can "brand" their food with their initials. Create a "saloon" on a side table, well stocked with beer and root beer and lots of shot glasses. Cover a bottle of whiskey or rum—the preferred Western alcohol—with a huge white "XXX" label. For the under-twenty-one cowpokes, serve iced tea in a jug labeled "Moonshine."

After dinner, if it's warm outside, you can set up the TV on the back porch with a long extension cord and hand out blankets and citronella candles. Adults can stretch out to enjoy a favorite Western epic while the kids toast marshmallows in the barbecue embers. At intermission, pass around the brown Betty, molasses-coffee chews, and cherry pie. To wash it all down, you might like to serve my version of "tobacco juice"—strong hot tea sweetened with molasses, laced with rum, and stirred with a licorice stick.

## Movie Suggestions

*The Alamo,* 1960. John Wayne stars in this story of Texas's fight for freedom in 1836.

*Annie Oakley,* 1935. Story of Buffalo Bill Cody and Annie Oakley, starring Barbara Stanwyck.

*Apache,* 1954. Stars Burt Lancaster as a Native American in Geronimo's army.

*Bad Company,* 1972. Drifters roam the West. Stars Jeff Bridges.

*Bad Day at Black Rock,* 1955. Spencer Tracy, Walter Brennan, Lee Marvin, and Ernest Borgnine star in this must-see Western.

*The Badlanders,* 1958. Double-crossing gold robbers.

*The Ballad of Little Jo,* 1993. Stars Ian McKellen and Heather Graham in a story of the gold rush.

*The Big Trail,* 1930. John Wayne's first starring role in a feature-length talkie.

*Billy the Kid,* 1941. Gunslinger tries to go straight.

*Blazing Saddles,* 1974. Western spoof by Mel Brooks. Not to be missed.

*The Bravados,* 1958. A sort of *Death Wish* set in the West. Stars Gregory Peck as a husband avenging his wife's murder.

*Butch Cassidy and the Sundance Kid,* 1969. Paul Newman and Robert Redford star in this classic about two lovable outlaws.

*Calamity Jane,* 1953. Musical Western starring Doris Day.

*Cat Ballou,* 1965. Western comedy starring Lee Marvin.

*City Slickers,* 1991. Comedy about a modern-day cattle drive, starring Billy Crystal.

*Dances with Wolves,* 1990. Directed by and starring Kevin Costner. Oscar-winning film about the West in 1870.

*Dodge City,* 1939. Stars Errol Flynn as sheriff.

*El Dorado,* 1967. John Wayne and James Caan star in a story about a frontier town.

*Flaming Star,* 1960. Set in 1870s Texas. Stars Elvis Presley.

*Fort Apache,* 1948. First in a classic trilogy about the West. Stars John Wayne, Shirley Temple, and Henry Fonda.

*Frontier Pony Express,* 1939. Stars Roy Rogers and his horse, Trigger.

*Geronimo: An American Legend,* 1993. Story of the Apache leader who fought the U.S. Army. Stars Robert Duvall and Gene Hackman.

*The Good, the Bad, and the Ugly,* 1966. Spaghetti Western starring Clint Eastwood and Eli Wallach. A must-see classic with terrific music.

*Gunfight at the O.K. Corral,* 1957. Burt Lancaster and Kirk Douglas star in the story of Wyatt Earp and Doc Holliday in Tombstone, Arizona.

*Gunfighter,* 1998. Martin Sheen stars in a story of the lawless West.

*High Noon,* 1952. Classic Western starring Gary Cooper, Grace Kelly, and Lon Chaney Jr.

*Hopalong Cassidy.* Series of movies made in the late thirties and forties starring William Boyd.

*How the West Was Won,* 1962. Classic Western with a star-studded cast, including John Wayne, Spencer Tracy, Gregory Peck, and James Stewart.

*Jeremiah Johnson,* 1972. Robert Redford stars as a man who wants to return to nature in this story set in 1830 in the West.

*The Last of the Mohicans,* 1992. Set in 1757. Stars Daniel Day-Lewis as a man raised by Mohicans.

*Little Big Man,* 1970. Dustin Hoffman stars in the story of a colorful gunslinger.

*Lone Star,* 1952. Action-packed Western starring Clark Gable and Ava Gardner.

*The Long Riders,* 1980. Story of Jesse James robbing banks, stagecoaches, and trains. Stars Dennis Quaid, Stacy Keach, and Keith Carradine.

*The Magnificent Seven,* 1960. Steve McQueen, Yul Brynner, and Charles Bronson star in the story of a Mexican town that hires gunmen to protect it.

*A Man Called Horse,* 1970. A white man endures torture to prove himself to a Sioux tribe.

*The Man Who Shot Liberty Valance,* 1962. Western starring John Wayne, in which he first uses his signature phrase, "Pilgrim."

*McCabe and Mrs. Miller,* 1971. Moving story of a western frontier brothel, starring Warren Beatty and Julie Christie.

*The Outlaw Josey Wales,* 1976. Clint Eastwood stars in this superb classic Western.

*Ride Him, Cowboy,* 1932. John Wayne and his white horse, Duke, star in the first of a series of six movies with the duo.

*Rio Bravo,* 1959. Stars John Wayne as a Texas sheriff.

*Rio Grande,* 1950. Third movie in a cavalry trilogy starring John Wayne.

*Shane,* 1953. Classic Western about a gunfighter who helps a frontier family. Stars Alan Ladd.

*She Wore a Yellow Ribbon,* 1949. John Wayne stars as a soon-to-retire cavalry officer.

*Silverado,* 1985. Star-studded Western with Kevin Kline, Kevin Costner, Danny Glover, and Jeff Goldblum.

*The Sons of Katie Elder,* 1965. John Wayne, Dean Martin, and Earl Holliman star as sons out to avenge their mother's death.

*True Grit,* 1969. John Wayne won his only career Oscar in this movie about a U.S. marshal hired to find a killer.

*Two Mules for Sister Sara,* 1969. Shirley MacLaine stars as a nun who joins hired gun Clint Eastwood.

*Unforgiven,* 1992. Clint Eastwood, Gene Hackman, and Morgan Freeman star in this must-see story of an aging gunslinger.

*Vera Cruz,* 1954. Action-packed Western starring Burt Lancaster and Gary Cooper.

*Way Out West,* 1937. Laurel and Hardy Western comedy.

*The Westerner,* 1940. Classic Western starring Gary Cooper and Walter Brennan.

*The Wild Bunch,* 1969. An absolute must-see Western starring William Holden and Ernest Borgnine.

*Wild Wild West,* 1999. Will Smith, Kevin Kline, and Kenneth Branagh star in the story of an evil inventor in the Old West.

*Wyatt Earp,* 1994. Kevin Costner and Dennis Quaid star in the story of Wyatt Earp.

# THE GILDED AGE

## FEATURE PRESENTATION

ENGLISH SCONES WITH PRESERVES ★ VICTORIAN TEA SANDWICHES

LEMON CAKE

## CLOSING CREDITS

SALLY LUNN CAKE ★ QUEEN VICTORIA'S CHERRY-ALMOND COOKIES

CHOCOLATE APRICOT DROPS ★ GINGER-LEMON ICES

PEACH MELBA ★ ORANGE BASKETS

## LIGHTS, CAMERA, ACTION! VICTORIAN TEA AND DESSERT PARTY

MOVIE SUGGESTIONS

The Victorian era is named for England's Queen Victoria, whose remarkably long reign lasted from 1837 to 1901. For the purposes of this chapter, I'm loosely defining it as the period of high society from the early 1800s to the start of World War I. As depicted in movies such as *Titanic,* this was a time of calling cards and letters of introduction, starched collars and high-laced corsets, croquet and garden parties, high tea and fancy dress balls. The Gilded Age, a term coined by Mark Twain, was a time of home-baked bread, with only 20 percent of the bread consumed in America being store-bought. It was a time when, according to *The Art of Entertaining,* an 1892 etiquette book, the ideal number of servants was eleven: a chef, a cook, a kitchen maid, a scullery servant, two laundresses, a parlor maid, and four "men." In those days before electric appliances, you really did need a houseful of servants. As we can see in Martin Scorsese's superbly researched *The Age of Innocence,* Victorian dinner parties were an elaborate affair that required a full staff to pull off.

A dinner party started with the invitations, which were handwritten and delivered by messenger at least ten days in advance. A hand-delivered reply was expected within twenty-four hours. Guests arrived precisely on time, as back then there was no such thing as being "fashionably late." Alcoholic beverages and hors d'oeuvres were not served as we do today;

instead everyone was seated for dinner fairly soon after arriving and then offered starters and drinks. Raw oysters were the favorite appetizer of the time, and they were often served on an attractive block of ice with lemon slices frozen inside, accompanied by a sweet wine like Sauternes.

The next course was usually turtle soup. A fish course, a meat course, and then a palate-cleansing sorbet before the game course followed. After that, assorted cheeses and crackers were served, followed by several choices of desserts, such as wine jellies, charlotte russe, meringue pies, cakes, and cream whipped with brandy topped with candied fruit. Finger bowls with flower petals floating in the water would be set in front of guests before they moved on to coffee and after-dinner drinks.

The following menu, perfect for a dessert party or afternoon high tea, is taken from various Gilded Age cookbooks. Two phenomenal cookie recipes are from Queen Victoria's chef, while the scrumptious tea sandwiches are from Fannie Farmer, who shaped a generation of American cooking. The wonderfully sweet-tart lemon cake comes from Catherine Beecher, whose sister, Harriet Beecher Stowe, wrote *Uncle Tom's Cabin*. There is a recipe for peach Melba created by Auguste Escoffier, one of Europe's finest chefs, who was awarded the Legion of Honour in 1920 for his culinary achievements.

So sit back—or rather, sit up straight—as we journey back to a time of gracious civility, impeccable manners, and elegant dining.

# ENGLISH SCONES WITH PRESERVES

*A group of colonists dressed as Red Indians boarded the vessel and dumped the tea overboard, making the tea unsuitable for drinking. Even for Americans!*

DAVID TOMLINSON, *MARY POPPINS*, 1964

☆  ☆  ☆

This recipe for moist, flavorful scones is from Isabella. Beeton, who in 1861, at age twenty-four, wrote a 1,000-plus-page cookbook that became England's leading culinary guide and Europe's bestselling cookbook.

Scones can be served with assorted preserves, lemon curd, or honey, and English clotted cream or crème fraîche. An elegant high tea essential that is perfect for brunch, too.

2 CUPS ALL-PURPOSE FLOUR

1 TABLESPOON SUGAR

¼ TEASPOON SALT

4 TABLESPOONS (½ STICK) COLD UNSALTED BUTTER, CUT INTO SMALL PIECES

½ TEASPOON BAKING SODA

½ CUP MILK

ASSORTED PRESERVES

1. Preheat the oven to 375 degrees.

2. In a large bowl, stir together the flour, sugar, and salt. Mix the butter into the dry ingredients with a fork or with your fingers until it is broken down into pea-sized lumps.

3. Stir in the baking soda and milk, mixing until the dough begins to come together. Turn the dough out onto a floured work surface and knead it briefly. Do not overwork the dough. It is supposed to be a little dry.

4. Pat the dough out into a 6-inch circle and cut it into 6 pie-shaped wedges. Transfer to a parchment-paper-lined baking sheet and bake for 12 to 14 minutes, until light golden.

5. Serve warm with assorted preserves.

*It left us speechless, quite speechless, I tell you, and we have not stopped talking of it since.* —SOPHIE THOMPSON, *EMMA*, 1996

Honeydew melons, kiwis, wild rice, and zucchini were not yet available in America's Gilded Age. There were no ice-cream cones, banana splits, or jelly beans either; they hadn't been invented yet. Although there were frankfurters, we didn't call them "hot dogs" then. There were no pizzerias, either—an Italian immigrant opened the first one in New York City in 1918.

# VICTORIAN TEA SANDWICHES

SERVES 6

*If you can't think of anything to say,*
*you will please restrict your remarks to the weather.*

GEMMA JONES, *SENSE AND SENSIBILITY*, 1995

☆  ☆  ☆

Teatime, the prototypical British social activity, is wonderfully depicted in the movie *Sense and Sensibility,* which tempts our taste buds with scenes of picnics, cotillions, and dinner parties. Emma Thompson, who stars in the film, wrote the screenplay, which is based on Jane Austen's novel. To get into an 1811 mind-set, Thompson reported, she covered up her TV, hid her radio, and canceled her newspaper delivery.

These sandwiches, which back then were served cut into triangles or into rounds using curly-edged cookie cutters, are typical of the assortment offered for high tea. For an added Victorian touch, garnish with radish roses, lemon zest, or edible flower petals.

8 THIN SLICES WHITE SANDWICH BREAD

4 THIN SLICES WHOLE WHEAT SANDWICH BREAD

6 TABLESPOONS (¾ STICK) BUTTER, SOFTENED

½ CUP THINLY SLICED CUCUMBER

¼ TEASPOON DRIED DILL

½ CUP GRATED GRUYÈRE CHEESE

⅓ CUP VERY FINELY CHOPPED WALNUTS

¼ TEASPOON CAYENNE PEPPER

½ PINT FRESH FIGS, CHOPPED

1 TEASPOON FRESHLY SQUEEZED LEMON JUICE

2 TABLESPOONS FINELY CHOPPED UNSALTED PEANUTS

1. Lay the white and whole wheat bread slices out on a work surface and butter each slice on one side.

2. To make cucumber sandwiches, place the sliced cucumber on 2 slices of the buttered white bread. Sprinkle with the dill and top each with another slice of the white bread, butter side down. Press each sandwich together lightly. With a sharp knife, remove the crusts and cut each sandwich into quarters. Transfer to a large platter.

3. To make Gruyère-walnut sandwiches, in a small bowl, stir together the Gruyère, walnuts, and cayenne until combined. Spoon the mixture onto 2 slices of the buttered white bread and top each with another slice of white bread, butter side down. Press each sandwich together lightly. With a sharp knife, remove the crusts and cut each sandwich into quarters. Place on the platter with the cucumber sandwiches.

4. To make fig-peanut sandwiches, in a small saucepan over low heat, simmer the figs with the lemon juice until very soft, about 12 minutes. Mash the figs with a fork and allow to cool. Spoon the mashed figs onto 2 slices of the buttered wheat bread and top each with 1 tablespoon of the peanuts. Top with the remaining 2 slices of the wheat bread, butter side down, and press each sandwich together lightly. With a sharp knife, remove the crusts and cut each sandwich into quarters. Add to the sandwich platter.

ORIGINAL RECIPE: FRUIT SANDWICHES — Remove stems and finely chop figs; add a small quantity of water, cook in double boiler until a paste is formed, then add a few drops of lemon juice. Cool mixture and spread on thin slices of buttered bread; sprinkle with finely chopped peanuts and cover with pieces of buttered bread.

— *THE BOSTON COOKING SCHOOL COOK BOOK*, 1896

> *You talk of feeling idle and useless. Imagine how that is compounded when one has no hope and no choice of any occupation whatsoever.* —EMMA THOMPSON, *SENSE AND SENSIBILITY*, 1995
>
> For one crucial scene during the filming of *Sense and Sensibility,* the director reportedly told actor Hugh Grant, "This is your big moment. I want to see your insides." To which the actor wryly replied, "Ah. Right-o. No pressure, then. . . ."

# LEMON CAKE

*Cake! Surely you're not serving cake at your wedding, Miss Taylor!*
*Far too rich, you put us all at peril!*

DENYS HAWTHORNE, *EMMA*, 1996

☆  ☆  ☆

This perfect, mouth-watering, lemony sweet-tart cake comes from the wildly successful 1846 cookbook by Catherine Beecher. In those days before thermometers, Miss Beecher had to be creative in explaining ways to judge proper oven temperature. Her advice in one case is, "If you cannot hold your hand in longer than to count twenty moderately, it is hot enough."

**CAKE**

8 TABLESPOONS (1 STICK) UNSALTED BUTTER, SOFTENED

1 CUP PLUS 2 TABLESPOONS GRANULATED SUGAR

4 LARGE EGGS, SEPARATED

JUICE AND GRATED ZEST OF 1 LARGE LEMON

2 TABLESPOONS BAKING POWDER

2 CUPS ALL-PURPOSE FLOUR

¼ CUP MILK, AT ROOM TEMPERATURE

**GLAZE**

1 CUP CONFECTIONERS' SUGAR

2 TABLESPOONS FRESHLY SQUEEZED LEMON JUICE

GRATED ZEST OF 1 LEMON

CANDIED VIOLETS (OPTIONAL)

1. Preheat the oven to 375 degrees. Butter and flour a 9-inch round pan and set aside.

2. In a mixing bowl, using an electric mixer set on high speed, blend the butter and the 1 cup granulated sugar together until light and fluffy, about 5 minutes. Add the egg yolks, one at a time, mixing well after each addition. Add the lemon juice, zest, and baking powder and mix well.

3. Slowly stir in the flour and milk. Mix on low speed until combined.

4. In another bowl, whip the egg whites with the electric mixer set on high. When the egg whites begin to get frothy, sprinkle with the 2 tablespoons granulated sugar. Continue beating until the egg whites form soft peaks.

5. Gently stir about one-quarter of the whites into the cake batter to lighten it. Fold in the remaining whites until just combined, being careful not to overmix. Pour the batter into the prepared pan and bake for about 30 minutes, or until golden and a toothpick inserted in the center comes out clean.

6. Allow the cake to cool on a rack in the pan for 10 minutes, then invert onto a serving platter and allow to cool completely.

7. To make the glaze, whisk together the confectioners' sugar and lemon juice until smooth. Pour half of the glaze over the top of the cooled cake, allowing it to drip down the sides. Allow the cake to stand for 10 minutes, then top with the remaining glaze.

8. Garnish with the lemon zest and candied violets, if using, and serve.

> *Carriages waited at the curb for the entire performance. It was widely known, in New York, but never acknowledged, that Americans want to get away from amusement even more quickly than they want to get to it.* —JOANNE WOODWARD, *THE AGE OF INNOCENCE*, 1993

The Gilded Age was a time of elegant entertainments, especially in socially important cities like New York, Philadelphia, and Newport, where the wealthy attended the theater, the opera, and concerts.

At home, the Victorian family enjoyed parlor games like dominoes, charades, and table croquet. Crafts such as "shard ware"—made from gluing broken pieces of china onto a surface—as well as needlepoint, sewing, knitting, dried-flower arranging, model building, and collecting were popular hobbies.

# SALLY LUNN CAKE

SERVES 10

*Perhaps some tea and cake would revive you.*

GRETA SCACCHI, *EMMA*, 1996

☆　☆　☆

There are several theories as to the origin of the name Sally Lunn cake. According to some, it comes from the French *Soleil Lune,* for "sun" and "moon," named after its shape. Others attribute it to an eighteenth-century woman named Sally Lunn who peddled her baked goods in the streets of Bath, England.

I question why this goody is called cake at all, since it's really more like moist white bread. Well, no matter what it's named, this easy-to-make, no-kneading-needed treat is excellent served right out of the oven with jam and the next day makes scrumptious sandwiches.

2 PACKAGES ACTIVE DRY YEAST

2 CUPS MILK, WARMED

4 CUPS ALL-PURPOSE FLOUR

1 TEASPOON SALT

3 LARGE EGGS, BEATEN

2 TABLESPOONS UNSALTED BUTTER, MELTED

JAM

WHIPPED CREAM (OPTIONAL)

1. Generously grease a 12-cup Bundt pan and set aside.

2. Sprinkle the yeast over the milk in a small bowl and stir to dissolve.

3. In a large bowl, stir together the flour and salt, making a well in the center. When the milk mixture begins to bubble, pour it into the flour along with the eggs and butter. Stir briskly until the batter is smooth. Pour into the prepared Bundt pan, cover, and allow to rise at room temperature for 1 hour.

4. Preheat the oven to 400 degrees.

5. Bake the cake for about 20 minutes, or until light golden. Allow to cool for 5 minutes in the pan, then invert onto a rack and allow to cool completely before cutting.

6. Serve with your favorite jam and whipped cream, if you'd like.

---

*That's the one good thing about Paris: There're a lot of girls willing to take their clothes off.*

—LEONARDO DICAPRIO, *TITANIC*, 1997

France's gift to America, the Statue of Liberty, is shown colored green in the movie *Titanic*. However, in 1912, the year *Titanic* sank, the statue was bright copper colored. It did not oxidize into its present green color until the 1940s.

# QUEEN VICTORIA'S CHERRY-ALMOND COOKIES

MAKES ABOUT 3 DOZEN COOKIES

*I am Queen Victoria, and I am very big in England!*
PETER SELLERS, *THE GREAT MCGONAGALL*, 1974

☆  ☆  ☆

Queen Victoria had a passion for cherries. Charles Francatelli, her chef, invented these buttery, light cherry cookies as well as cherries jubilee to celebrate the queen's diamond jubilee in 1897. The dough for these delicious cookies keeps for several days in the fridge, so these are great make-ahead treats.

¼ CUP DRIED CHERRIES

¼ CUP GRANULATED SUGAR

8 TABLESPOONS (1 STICK) UNSALTED BUTTER, SOFTENED

¾ CUP ALL-PURPOSE FLOUR

¼ CUP VERY FINELY CHOPPED ALMONDS

PINCH OF SALT

CONFECTIONERS' SUGAR

1. Preheat the oven to 375 degrees. Line a baking sheet with parchment paper and set aside.

2. Grind the cherries and granulated sugar in a food processor until the cherries are finely chopped.

3. In a large bowl, cream the butter with an electric mixer until fluffy. Add the cherry-sugar mixture and blend until well combined. Add the flour, almonds, and salt and mix on low speed until combined. Turn the dough out onto a piece of parchment paper or plastic wrap and shape into a log about ¾ inch in diameter. Roll it on the counter to smooth the edges. Chill for at least 30 minutes and up to 3 days.

4. When ready to bake, slice the dough into ⅓-inch slices and place 1 inch apart on the lined baking sheet. Bake for about 10 minutes, or until the edges are light golden. Allow the cookies to cool on the baking sheet before removing.

5. Arrange on a serving platter and sprinkle with confectioners' sugar.

*It's grand to be an Englishman in 1910.*
*King Edward's on the thrown,*
*it's the age of men!*
—DAVID TOMLINSON, *MARY POPPINS*, 1964

Besides cherries jubilee, other dishes created in the Victorian era include brownies, oysters Rockefeller (named after the wealthy John D. Rockefeller), hamburgers, and Waldorf salad, created by maître d' Oscar Tschirky, at New York's famed Waldorf-Astoria Hotel.

# CHOCOLATE APRICOT DROPS

SERVES 8

*May I tell you what most interests me about New York? Not all the blind obeying of tradition—somebody else's tradition. It seems stupid to have discovered America only to make it a copy of another country.*

MICHELLE PFEIFFER, *THE AGE OF INNOCENCE*, 1993

☆　☆　☆

This recipe for tiny chocolaty cookies dotted with apricot jam was invented by a Gilded Age chef at New York's famed Delmonico's Restaurant and created for socialite Caroline Astor.

Both Henry James and Edith Wharton depicted wealthy Victorians in their novels, many of which, such as *The Portrait of a Lady, The Heiress, Ethan Frome,* and *The Age of Innocence,* have been made into movies.

8 TABLESPOONS (1 STICK) UNSALTED BUTTER, SOFTENED

½ CUP PACKED DARK BROWN SUGAR

1 LARGE EGG

1 TEASPOON VANILLA EXTRACT

½ CUP UNSWEETENED COCOA POWDER

1½ CUPS ALL-PURPOSE FLOUR

PINCH OF SALT

GRANULATED SUGAR

½ CUP APRICOT PRESERVES

1. Preheat the oven to 375 degrees.

2. In a mixing bowl, using an electric mixer set on high speed, blend the butter and brown sugar together until light and fluffy, about 5 minutes. Add the egg and vanilla and mix well. Reduce the mixer speed to low and add the cocoa powder, mixing until combined and smooth. Slowly add ¾ cup of the flour until a stiff dough begins to form. Add the remaining ¾ cup flour and the salt and stir with a spoon until well combined.

3. Take about 1 teaspoonful of dough and form it into a ball about ¾ inch in diameter. Roll the ball in granulated sugar and place on a parchment-paper-lined baking sheet. Repeat with the remaining dough. Using your pinky, make a small indent in the center of each cookie. Fill each cookie center with a bit of the apricot preserves.

4. Bake for about 10 minutes, or until the cookies are set. Serve warm or cool.

---

*Please, sir, I want some more.*

—MARK LESTER, *OLIVER!*, 1968

The nineteenth century was a time of many great writers like Jane Austen, Arthur Conan Doyle, Mary Shelley, Mark Twain, Edgar Allan Poe, and George Bernard Shaw, all of whose novels have been made into films.

Charles Dickens alone inspired more than fifty movies, including such classics as *A Christmas Carol, David Copperfield, Great Expectations, The Life and Adventures of Nicholas Nickleby, Oliver!, Scrooge,* and *A Tale of Two Cities.*

# GINGER-LEMON ICES

SERVES 6

*Do you know of Dr. Freud? . . . His ideas of the male preoccupation*
*with size might be of particular interest to you.*

KATE WINSLET, *TITANIC,* 1997

☆  ☆  ☆

Members of high society, who paid the present-day equivalent of $75,000 for a first-class suite on the *Titanic,* were served lavish meals that included flavored ices as between-course palate cleansers. This light and refreshing ice also creates an elegant finish to any meal. The recipe comes from an ex-slave who worked in posh dining cars during the Gilded Age and then published a cookbook of his innovations.

2 CUPS SUGAR

5 LEMONS

3 TABLESPOONS MINCED CANDIED GINGER

1. Combine the sugar with 4 cups of water in a saucepan over high heat. Bring to a boil, reduce the heat to medium, and simmer for 15 minutes.

2. Meanwhile, grate the zest of 2 of the lemons and reserve. Juice all 5 of the lemons; you should get about 1 cup of juice. Using a spoon, remove any remaining pulp from the 6 unpeeled lemon halves. Cut about ¼ inch off the ends of the lemon halves so they will sit upright. Place them on a plate and freeze.

3. Once the sugar water has simmered for 15 minutes, add the grated zest, lemon juice, and ginger and stir. Pour the mixture into a shallow metal or plastic cake pan and freeze for 1 hour. Stir the mixture with a fork to break up any large crystals. Repeat every 30 minutes until the mixture is completely frozen into very small crystals.

4. To serve, spoon the ginger-lemon ice into the frozen lemon cups.

**ORIGINAL RECIPE: LEMON-GINGER SHERBET** — This is made the same as the lemon with the addition of four ounces of candied ginger cut in fine bits and added to the sirrup [*sic*] with the grated yellow rind of a lemon. Boil until clear, add lemon juice and a little more of the rind and proceed as with the ice.

*— GOOD THINGS TO EAT,* 1911

> *Yes, we have no bananas!*
>
> —FRANK SILVER AND IRVING COHN, 1923
>
> Bananas, introduced into America during the mid-1800s, were considered so elegant that special gondola-shaped "banana bowls" were created to serve them at dinner parties. Celery and oranges each had a specific serving plate back then, too.

# PEACH MELBA

SERVES 6

☆  ☆  ☆

Although the singer Julie Andrews played Eliza Doolittle on Broadway to rave reviews, the producers were worried that she might not be enough of a box office draw for the film version of *My Fair Lady.* Audrey Hepburn was cast, but the songs were sung by Marni Nixon, who also dubbed songs for Natalie Wood in *West Side Story* and Deborah Kerr in *The King and I.*

The world-renowned French chef Auguste Escoffier created this luscious treat, named after Gilded Age opera singer Dame Nellie Melba. In this modern version I don't bother peeling the peaches, which helps them keep their shape and adds a nice texture to this classic dessert.

3 LARGE PEACHES

2 CUPS PLUS 3 TABLESPOONS SUGAR

1 TABLESPOON VANILLA EXTRACT

ONE 10-OUNCE BAG FROZEN RASPBERRIES, THAWED

1 PINT VANILLA ICE CREAM

1. Halve the peaches and remove the pits. Reserve the peach halves. In a large saucepan, bring 3 cups of water and the 2 cups sugar to a rolling boil. Add the vanilla extract and peach halves, cut side down, to the saucepan. Remove from the heat and cover. Allow the peaches to steep in the liquid until softened, about 20 minutes.

2. Meanwhile, puree the raspberries and the 3 tablespoons sugar in a blender. Pass the puree through a mesh strainer to remove the seeds. Reserve the raspberry puree.

3. To serve, remove the warm peach halves from the vanilla syrup and place, cut side up, on 6 dessert plates. Top each peach with a small scoop of the ice cream and drizzle the raspberry sauce over the top.

*Why can't a woman be more like a man?* —REX HARRISON, *MY FAIR LADY*, 1964

Cary Grant, Noël Coward, and Michael Redgrave were all considered for the part of Professor Henry Higgins. Although this is a love story, movie buffs observe that no one in this movie ever kisses.

# ORANGE BASKETS

SERVES 4

*It's better to be looked over than overlooked.*

MAE WEST, *BELLE OF THE NINETIES*, 1934

☆　☆　☆

Many new inventions debuted at the Chicago World's Fair in 1893, including a two-sided electric griddle, a chocolate-making machine, and the Ferris wheel, a marvel of engineering that was the fair's star attraction.

New foods were introduced, too, including shredded wheat, Pabst Blue Ribbon beer, Mott's apple cider, Aunt Jemima pancake syrup, Poland Spring water, and Juicy Fruit chewing gum. Foods were used to construct fanciful displays at the fair such as a huge map of the United States made of pickles, complete with vinegar lakes and rivers; a copy of the Liberty Bell in various grains; a chocolate Venus de Milo; a raisin pyramid; and a globe made with over 6,000 oranges that had to be replaced every few days to keep the exhibit fresh.

In the 1880s, a popular dessert was orange-flavored gelatin served in baskets carved from oranges. For this modern version, I've filled the carved oranges with fresh fruit and a splash of liqueur. A refreshingly light dessert that makes a gorgeous addition to any party buffet table.

4 LARGE NAVEL ORANGES

1 PINT STRAWBERRIES, SLICED

DASH OF ORANGE LIQUEUR, SUCH AS COINTREAU

ORGANIC LEAVES, SUCH AS ORANGE, MINT, OR BAY LEAF (OPTIONAL)

1. With a sharp knife, cut about ¼ inch off the navel end of each orange so that it will sit upright. Cut 2 equal-sized wedges out of the top half of the orange, leaving a ½-inch-wide handle intact. Trim the flesh away from the peel, taking care not to tear the handle, then, using a spoon, remove the flesh from the bowl of the orange basket.

2. Reserve the orange flesh, cutting off all the white membranes, and mix in a bowl with the strawberries. Toss with the orange liqueur and fill the baskets.

3. To serve, arrange leaves, if using, on a serving plate and top with an orange basket. For an additional garnish, tie a ribbon onto the handle of the basket.

ORIGINAL RECIPE: ORANGE BASKETS—Cut as many oranges as will be required, leaving half the peel whole for the baskets, and a strip half an inch wide for the handle. Remove the pulp and juice, and use the juice in making orange jelly. Place the baskets in a pan of broken ice to keep upright. Fill with orange jelly. When ready to serve, put a spoonful of whipped cream over the jelly in each basket. Serve in a bed of orange or laurel leaves.

—*MRS. LINCOLN'S BOSTON COOK BOOK*, 1883

*. . . The corn flake is my gift to the entire world.* —ANTHONY HOPKINS, *THE ROAD TO WELLVILLE*, 1994

The second half of the 1800s gave us a slew of health food advocates. Many focused on breakfast, such as the Reverend Sylvester Graham, promoter of whole wheat "graham" flour; Dr. James Jackson, the inventor of granola; C. W. Post, the creator of Grape-Nuts cereal; and the Kellogg brothers, promoters of cornflakes as a breakfast food.

Dr. John Kellogg, who started a Battle Creek, Michigan, health sanatorium, ended up in a court battle against his brother Will concerning who had the rights to the family name. Will won, which is why his signature is in big red letters on every box of Kellogg's Corn Flakes.

# VICTORIAN TEA AND DESSERT PARTY

Apart from fond childhood memories of my toy china set, I love tea and dessert parties for two reasons: First, they are a great way to host a large group of friends without the fuss of preparing a whole meal, and second, they allow me to entertain at unusual hours, like after the theater or on Sunday afternoons.

During the Gilded Age, five o'clock tea, or high tea, as it was called in England, was served from special tea wagons, which had fold-down flaps for guests to set their cups, as well as plenty of compartments for the tea service and nibbles. If you are serving tea to a small group in the living room, any side table covered with a tablecloth can serve as a tea cart. It is very Gilded Age for extra fabric to gather at the bottom, so don't worry if the tablecloth is too big. For large groups, though, you'll probably want to set up on the kitchen or dining room table.

Popular then were parties with color themes, where the guests would be asked to dress in a particular color that coordinated with the food and decorations, so you can opt for all one color if you like. I prefer the rainbow approach and like to mix and match cups, saucers, plates, and teapots. If you aren't too concerned about chips or buying a complete matching set, you can pick up some wonderful pieces at tag sales, flea markets, and antiques shops. I mix early 1900s lusterware saucers with modern china cups, and Fiestaware dessert plates with cracked, but gorgeous, Wedgwood and transfer ware plates.

Since the Victorians were such avid collectors, this is a great occasion to decorate the table with your favorite collectibles. I collect obsolete objects and arrange an assortment of Victorian oddities like mother-of-pearl dance cards (so ladies could keep track of dance partners), snuffboxes, butter presses (to decorate squares of fresh-churned butter), mustache cups (with ceramic barriers to keep 1890s handlebar mustaches dry), posy holders, horseradish spoons (during the Gilded Age, almost every food had its own particular utensil), pickle forks, and spoon warmers (yes, they heated utensils in attractive hot-water holders so spoons wouldn't cool the hot drinks).

A very Victorian touch is decorated sugar cubes. A few tubes of icing gel can unleash the artist within, or you can buy already decorated sugar cubes in specialty shops. In addition to your favorite flavors of tea, you might like to serve dessert wine or champagne at your dessert party. Or, as was done at the time, you can serve sweet cordials or port. After dinner, Victorian ladies would leave the table to allow the men the opportunity to smoke cigars before joining them for cordials in the library or drawing room.

A popular recipe of the time for homemade cherry cordial mixed $2\frac{1}{2}$ pounds of pitted cherries with a quart of brandy and left the mixture to rest in a sealed jug for two weeks. Then 1 pound of sugar was boiled in $\frac{3}{4}$ cup of water until dissolved. Once cooled, it was added to the brandy, which was then strained just before serving. The results were sensational, and I've had success not just with cherries, but also with Concord grapes and raspberries. So raise your glasses and let's toast to the past with one of the popular toasts of 1899, "Long life, pure love, and boundless liberty." Cheers!

## Movie Suggestions

*The Adventures of Sherlock Holmes,* 1939. Classic story of the invincible sleuth, starring Basil Rathbone.

*The Age of Innocence,* 1993. Movie based on Edith Wharton's novel set in 1870s New York, starring Michelle Pfeiffer and Winona Ryder.

*Angels and Insects,* 1995. Interesting Gilded Age tale of lust and incest.

*Anna Karenina,* 1935. Greta Garbo and Basil Rathbone star in this Russian tale.

*The Barretts of Wimpole Street,* 1934. Story of Victorian-era poets Elizabeth Barrett and Robert Browning. Stars Fredric March and Maureen O'Sullivan.

*Beau Brummell,* 1954. Elizabeth Taylor and Peter Ustinov star in the story of George Brummell, who becomes friends with England's King George III.

*Belle of the Nineties,* 1934. Stars Mae West as a Gay Nineties singer.

*Bride of Frankenstein,* 1935. Based on Mary Shelley's novel, starring Boris Karloff.

*David Copperfield,* 1935. Based on the Charles Dickens novel, starring Lionel Barrymore and W. C. Fields.

*A Doll's House,* 1973. Jane Fonda stars in Ibsen's classic about a Victorian-era woman's desire for freedom.

*The Elephant Man,* 1980. Movie based on the true Victorian-era story of the severely deformed John Merrick. Stars John Hurt, Anthony Hopkins, and Anne Bancroft.

*Emma,* 1996. Gwyneth Paltrow stars in this movie, based on a Jane Austen novel.

*Ethan Frome,* 1993. Edith Wharton's novel, starring Liam Neeson and Patricia Arquette.

*The Europeans,* 1979. Lee Remick stars in this movie, based on the novel by Henry James.

*Frankenstein.* The classic Gothic tale inspired by Mary Shelley's novel has been made into various films, including the 1931 classic, starring Boris Karloff; the 1943 version with the Wolf Man, starring Lon Chaney Jr. and Bela Lugosi; and a 1982 version with Carrie Fisher.

*The French Lieutenant's Woman,* 1981. Meryl Streep stars as an 1800s woman with secrets.

*Funny Girl,* 1968. Stars Barbra Streisand as Fanny Brice, the early 1900s star of the Ziegfeld Follies.

*Gaslight,* 1944. Charles Boyer tries to drive his wife, Ingrid Bergman, insane by, among other things, fiddling with the gas-powered lights in the house (set in the days before electric dimmers!).

*Great Expectations,* 1946. Must-see movie based on the Charles Dickens novel, starring Alec Guinness.

*The Great Train Robbery,* 1979. Set aboard an 1855 luxury train, starring Sean Connery and Donald Sutherland.

*The Heiress,* 1949. Olivia de Havilland stars as a plain but wealthy Victorian spinster.

*The Importance of Being Earnest,* 2002. Comedy based on Oscar Wilde's play, starring Reese Witherspoon, Judi Dench, and Colin Firth.

*Jane Eyre,* 1996. Based on Charlotte Brontë's novel about a shy governess. Stars William Hurt and Anna Paquin.

*Life with Father*, 1947. Set in 1880s New York, starring Elizabeth Taylor.

*The Little Princess*, 1939. Shirley Temple stars as an orphan in Victorian London.

*Little Women*, 1933. Based on the novel about four sisters by Louisa May Alcott. Stars Katharine Hepburn and Joan Bennett.

*Little Women*, 1994. Remake starring Susan Sarandon and Winona Ryder.

*Mary Poppins*, 1964. Julie Andrews in her film debut as a magical nanny in turn-of-the-century England.

*Moulin Rouge!*, 2001. Set in 1899 Paris. Stars Nicole Kidman.

*My Fair Lady*, 1964. Musical starring Audrey Hepburn and Rex Harrison.

*Oliver!*, 1968. Musical based on the Charles Dickens novel.

*Oliver Twist*, 1948. The Charles Dickens story of an orphan in Victorian England.

*The Portrait of a Lady*, 1996. Movie based on Henry James's novel, starring Nicole Kidman and John Malkovich.

*Pride and Prejudice*, 1940. Oscar-winning movie based on Jane Austen's novel. Stars Laurence Olivier.

*The Secret Garden*, 1993. Based on F. H. Burnett's classic tale of a neglected garden.

*Sense and Sensibility*, 1995. Jane Austen's novel adapted by and starring Emma Thompson.

*Shanghai Noon*, 2000. The Wild West meets Victorian England. Comedy starring Jackie Chan and Owen Wilson.

*The Story of Alexander Graham Bell,* 1939. Henry Fonda and Don Ameche star in this story of the inventor of the telephone.

*Time After Time*, 1979. Story of time-machine travel, set in Victorian London.

*Titanic*, 1997. Oscar-sweeping love story set on the *Titanic.* Stars Leonardo DiCaprio and Kate Winslet.

*Topsy-Turvy*, 1999. Story of the musical team Gilbert and Sullivan, set in England circa 1885.

*Uncle Tom's Cabin*, 1987. Excellent made-for-TV movie based on Harriet Beecher Stowe's novel.

*Wuthering Heights*, 1939. Based on Emily Brontë's romantic classic. Stars Laurence Olivier.

# THE WAR YEARS

**COMING ATTRACTIONS**

VICTORY GARDEN SALAD ★ WORLD WAR I POTATO SOUP

**FEATURE PRESENTATION**

CHEESE RAREBIT ★ CREAMY SHREDDED BEEF WITH ALMONDS

TUNA À LA KING ★ PEANUT AND CHEESE MACARONI ★ "WOOLWORTH SPECIAL"

**CLOSING CREDITS**

MAPLE-GLAZED ANGEL FOOD CAKE

PEPPERMINT DEVIL'S FOOD SQUARES ★ JAM TRIANGLES

**LIGHTS, CAMERA, ACTION! COMFORT FOODS POTLUCK SUPPER**

MOVIE SUGGESTIONS

Hollywood has created hundreds of war films, and whether you are a hawk, a dove, or don't have a peep of an opinion, these films are some of the most important in moviemaking history. Some, such as *Platoon* and *Saving Private Ryan,* realistically depict battle; several, such as *M\*A\*S\*H,* make humorous antiwar statements; and still others, such as *Schindler's List* and *Life Is Beautiful,* have life-affirming themes.

This chapter offers a glimpse into the changes that World War I and World War II brought to our tables and includes a range of sugarless, meatless, and eggless recipes developed to cope with rationing and shortages.

At the start of World War II, the secretary of agriculture issued a message to Americans urging consumers to "let patriotism dictate your shopping list. . . . Buy what is plentiful, buy what is fresh, buy what is produced locally and . . . do not hoard." During World War II, despite all attempts to prevent it, the government instituted mandatory food rationing for the first time in America's history. The first food to be rationed was sugar, quickly followed by meat, butter, and coffee.

Ladies' magazines, government pamphlets, and cookbooks discussed ways to make the most of limited ration points. One classic cookbook of the time was M.F.K. Fisher's *How to*

*Cook a Wolf,* which included chapters such as "How to Be Cheerful Though Starving," "How to Be Sage Without Hemlock," and "How Not to Boil an Egg."

It wasn't only rationing and shortages that dictated meals, but time available in the kitchen, too. Women joined the workforce in record numbers to fill the jobs left by men now in the military. Cooking shortcuts and convenience foods became increasingly necessary to cope with the new workingwoman's lifestyle.

The following tasty family-pleasing recipes are a sample of the affordable comfort foods of the forties.

# VICTORY GARDEN SALAD

SERVES 8

*Get your mind out of the sports section and onto the front page.*

WILLIAM DEMAREST, *ALL THROUGH THE NIGHT*, 1942

☆ ☆ ☆

During World War II, newspapers across America published gardening hints and awarded war bonds to innovative home gardeners. By 1945, over 40 percent of America's vegetables were grown in backyard and window-box "Victory Gardens." Growing and eating veggies was viewed as a patriotic act, and canning became a craze, with the average American family "putting up" 165 quarts of vegetables a year. This modern cucumber salad has all the flavors of homemade pickles without the fuss of jars and sterilizing.

¾ CUP WHITE VINEGAR

⅓ CUP PACKED LIGHT BROWN SUGAR

2 TABLESPOONS PICKLING SPICE (SEE NOTE)

1 TABLESPOON SALT

1 SMALL PURPLE ONION, SLICED

3 GARLIC CLOVES, PEELED

4 KIRBY CUCUMBERS, SLICED

1 RED BELL PEPPER, THINLY SLICED

1. In a small saucepan, bring the vinegar, brown sugar, pickling spice, and salt to a boil over medium-high heat. Add the onion and garlic and remove from the heat. Cool completely.

2. Put the cucumbers and bell pepper into a serving bowl and pour the pickling mixture over the top, tossing lightly to coat. Serve within 2 days.

NOTE: If you prefer to make the pickling seasoning yourself, use 1½ teaspoons whole allspice, 1 teaspoon red pepper flakes, 10 whole cloves, ¼ teaspoon mustard seed, ⅛ teaspoon ground coriander, and ⅛ teaspoon ground cinnamon.

> *I'm gonna ride you till you can't stand up. And when you do stand up, you're gonna be Marines.*
>
> —JOHN WAYNE, *SANDS OF IWO JIMA*, 1949

The Armour Company, which supplied emergency K rations for the military, gave free pamphlets to worried mothers and wives wanting to know what their men were eating at the front. The 8-ounce boxes of U.S. Army K-ration dinners contained processed cheese, enriched crackers, a tube of concentrated soup, graham crackers, a vitamin-enriched chocolate bar, and chewing gum.

John Wayne, who shared many a ration while visiting the troops for the USO, represented every branch of the military in his 170-plus films. The army even named a helicopter *Duke*, after him.

# WORLD WAR I POTATO SOUP

SERVES 8

*Seeing as how the VP is such a VIP, shouldn't we keep the PC on the QT?*
*'Cause of the leaks to VC, he could end up MIA, and then we'd all be put out in KP.*
ROBIN WILLIAMS, *GOOD MORNING, VIETNAM*, 1987

☆  ☆  ☆

This creamy, family-satisfying soup comes from a World War I army cooks' manual. Although the original calls for peeled potatoes, in this modern version I've substituted unpeeled red new potatoes. Cuts down on KP, and looks fabulous.

3 TABLESPOONS BUTTER

1 LARGE ONION, DICED

¼ CUP ALL-PURPOSE FLOUR

2 POUNDS RED NEW POTATOES, DICED

4 CUPS BEEF STOCK

1 CUP HEAVY CREAM

SALT AND PEPPER

3 BACON STRIPS, COOKED AND CRUMBLED

1 TABLESPOON DRIED CHIVES

CAYENNE PEPPER

1.  In a large pot, melt the butter over medium heat. Add the onion and cook until softened, about 5 minutes. Sprinkle the flour over the onion and cook, stirring, until incorporated. Add the potatoes and stock and bring to a boil. Reduce the heat to maintain a simmer and cook until the potatoes are tender, about 15 minutes. Stir in the heavy cream, season with salt and pepper to taste, and cook until hot but not boiling.

2.  To serve, ladle the soup into individual bowls and top each with bacon, chives, and a pinch of cayenne.

*Today President Lyndon Johnson passed a highway beautification bill. The bill basically said that his daughters could not drive in a convertible on public highways.* —ROBIN WILLIAMS, *GOOD MORNING, VIETNAM*, 1987

During World War II, many ads encouraged conservation of gasoline with slogans like "When you ride alone, you ride with Hitler—join a car-sharing club today!"

# CHEESE RAREBIT

SERVES 6

*—Something wrong with your meal, Carney?*

*—Yes, Sergeant, it's the first food I was ever afraid of.*

CHRISTOPHER WALKEN AND CASEY SIEMASZKO, *BILOXI BLUES*, 1988

☆　☆　☆

Welsh rarebit, a nineteenth-century English specialty, was adopted as America's ultimate comfort food during World War II. Originally made with Cheddar cheese melted in ale and seasoned with mustard, this veggie-packed version—called Mexican rarebit back then—can be sent even further south of the border with jalapeño peppers.

| | |
|---|---|
| 2 TABLESPOONS BUTTER | ½ TEASPOON TABASCO SAUCE |
| 1 GREEN BELL PEPPER, FINELY CHOPPED | ½ TEASPOON GROUND CUMIN |
| 1 SMALL PURPLE ONION, DICED | 3 CUPS GRATED MONTEREY JACK CHEESE |
| 2 TABLESPOONS ALL-PURPOSE FLOUR | SALT AND PEPPER |
| ¾ CUP MILK | 6 TORTILLAS, WARMED |
| 1 LARGE TOMATO, DICED | DICED JALAPEÑO PEPPER (OPTIONAL) |
| 1 TEASPOON CHILI POWDER | |

1. In a large skillet, melt the butter over medium heat. Add the bell pepper and onion and cook until softened, about 5 minutes. Sprinkle in the flour, stir, and cook for 2 minutes. Add the milk and continue cooking until thickened, about 4 minutes. Reduce the heat to low and stir in the tomato, chili powder, Tabasco sauce, and cumin until combined. Add the Monterey Jack and stir until melted and smooth. Season to taste with salt and pepper.

2. Serve with the warm tortillas, and garnish with diced jalapeño pepper, if desired.

---

*I thought I would stand up here and let you people see if I am as big a son of a bitch as some of you think I am.* —GEORGE C. SCOTT, *PATTON*, 1970

*Patton,* winner of eight Academy Awards, including Best Picture, stars George C. Scott as General George S. Patton Jr.

Patton, affectionately referred to as "Old Blood and Guts" by his men, was a controversial figure. He once raised tremendous public outrage for slapping a hospitalized soldier suffering from shell shock.

George C. Scott caused controversy of his own when he became the first actor to refuse to accept his Oscar, claiming that he did not approve of competition between actors.

# CREAMY SHREDDED BEEF WITH ALMONDS

SERVES 6

*If they ever dropped this stuff over Germany,*
*the entire country would come out with their hands up.*

A DRAFTEE, *BILOXI BLUES*, 1988

☆　☆　☆

Meatless Tuesdays were a short-lived campaign during World War II, instituted to encourage civilians to self-limit meat consumption to avoid shortages. Butchers, however, reported no drop in sales, so the plan was scratched and meat rationing begun in March 1943.

Shredded dehydrated beef, cooked into creamy stews and served over toast, became a military and civilian staple, jokingly called "shit on a shingle" by the men in uniform. Jokes aside, this much-maligned dish tastes great, especially when you use a highly flavorful Italian cold cut such as bresaola or prosciutto, available in most supermarkets and at Italian specialty grocers.

2 TABLESPOONS BUTTER, PLUS MORE AS NEEDED

1 SMALL PURPLE ONION, THINLY SLICED

5 OUNCES BRESAOLA OR PROSCIUTTO, THINLY MINCED

2 TABLESPOONS ALL-PURPOSE FLOUR

1½ CUPS MILK

2 CELERY STALKS, FINELY DICED

1 TABLESPOON WORCESTERSHIRE SAUCE

SALT AND PEPPER

BUTTERED TOASTED BAGUETTE SLICES

2 TABLESPOONS SLICED ALMONDS

1. In a large skillet, melt the 2 tablespoons butter over medium heat. Add the onion and cook until softened, about 4 minutes. Add the meat and sprinkle the flour over the mixture. Cook, stirring, until the flour is incorporated, about 2 minutes. Add the milk, celery, and Worcestershire sauce and simmer until thick, 2 to 3 minutes. Season to taste with salt and pepper.

2. Serve warm over buttered toasted baguette slices, topped with the sliced almonds.

*Yankee Doodle Floppy Disk, this is Foxtrot Zulu Milkshake,*

*checking in at 700 feet, request permission to land.*

—KEVIN DUNN, *HOT SHOTS!*, 1991

While I was studying for my pilot's license I learned that all air traffic controllers and pilots, regardless of their native language, must speak English during radio communications at international airports. To avoid confusion due to alphabet pronunciation differences among nationalities, an international system was devised whereby each letter is represented by a specific word: *A* is "Alpha," *B* "Bravo," *C* "Charlie," and so forth. In *Hot Shots!*, the fighter-pilot spoof, they did get a few of the letters right—*Z* is "Zulu," and *F* really is "Foxtrot."

# TUNA À LA KING

SERVES 4

*Sir, I've inspected this boat,*
*and I think you ought to know that I can't swim.*
DAVID NIVEN, *THE GUNS OF NAVARONE*, 1961

☆　☆　☆

Chicken à la king was created at the posh New York City restaurant Delmonico's in the 1920s. This creamy tuna version, from *Thrifty Cooking for War Time* by Alice Winn-Smith, was developed as an inexpensive and easy-to-prepare World War II alternative. You can serve it on toast, as was done then, or over buttered noodles or rice.

2 TABLESPOONS BUTTER

½ SMALL ONION, MINCED

½ GREEN BELL PEPPER, MINCED

1 CARROT, GRATED

3 TABLESPOONS ALL-PURPOSE FLOUR

2 CUPS MILK

1½ TEASPOONS SALT

PINCH OF CAYENNE PEPPER

PINCH OF GROUND NUTMEG

12 OUNCES OIL- OR WATER-PACKED TUNA,
    DRAINED

1 TABLESPOON CHOPPED FRESH PARSLEY

BUTTERED TOAST, NOODLES, OR RICE

1.  In a large saucepan, melt the butter over medium heat. Add the onion, bell pepper, and carrot and cook until the vegetables are softened, about 4 minutes. Sprinkle the flour over the vegetables and continue cooking, stirring constantly, for another 2 minutes. Add the milk, salt, cayenne, and nutmeg and bring to a boil. Stir in the tuna and parsley. Reduce the heat to medium and simmer until thick, 2 to 3 minutes.

2.  Serve over buttered toast, noodles, or rice.

# PEANUT AND CHEESE MACARONI

SERVES 8

*—Looks like enemy aircraft at twelve o'clock.*

*—Really? Twelve o'clock? Well, that gives us about . . . twenty-five minutes.*

*Think I'll step out for a burger.*

JON CRYER AND LLOYD BRIDGES, *HOT SHOTS!*, 1991

☆ ☆ ☆

Due to meat rationing and shortages in the 1940s, America reached an all-time high in egg and milk consumption. "Meatless dishes for victory dinners" became the slogan for patriotic meals such as this delicious variation on the usual macaroni and cheese. Peanuts add flavor and crunch to this simple-to-make crowd-pleaser.

1 POUND ELBOW MACARONI

1 SMALL RED ONION, FINELY DICED

½ CUP MILK

4 TABLESPOONS (½ STICK) BUTTER

8 OUNCES AMERICAN CHEESE, CUBED

¾ CUP UNSALTED PEANUTS

½ CUP SEASONED DRIED BREAD CRUMBS

½ PINT CHERRY TOMATOES, HALVED

SALT AND PEPPER

1. Bring a large pot of salted water to a boil over high heat. Cook the macaroni according to package directions until al dente. Drain and immediately toss the onion with the hot macaroni in the colander.

2. Meanwhile, heat the milk and butter in a large saucepan over medium heat until the butter is melted. Add the cheese and cook, stirring, until melted and smooth.

3. Pulse the peanuts and bread crumbs together in a food processor until coarse. Transfer to a small dry nonstick skillet over medium-low heat and toast, stirring, until light golden, about 2 minutes.

4. Stir the pasta into the cheese sauce until well coated. Add the tomatoes and season to taste with salt and pepper.

5. Serve warm topped with the toasted crumb mixture.

---

*This is my story. This is the sacrifice my father made. This was his gift to me.*

—ROBERTO BENIGNI, *LIFE IS BEAUTIFUL*, 1998

Roberto Benigni won an Academy Award for Best Actor for his role in *Life Is Beautiful,* a film he directed. Benigni is only the second actor ever to direct himself to an Oscar. The first was Laurence Olivier in 1949 for *Hamlet.* Interestingly, neither one is American.

# "WOOLWORTH SPECIAL"

SERVES 8

*Now I know why drugstores have lunch counters. They lose a lot of money
on food and make a big profit on bicarbonate of soda.*

DEANNA DURBIN, *IT STARTED WITH EVE*, 1941

☆  ☆  ☆

This recipe comes from *Parties for Pennies,* a 1942 cookbook by Nancy Webb that boasted ways for "bank-accountless" civilians to entertain "soldier and sailor friends on leave." The dish was named after the now-defunct five-and-ten store chain Woolworth's, which served inexpensive lunch-counter meals.

This satisfying one-pot meal is a snap to make, and kids love it.

1 PURPLE ONION, DICED

3 TABLESPOONS OLIVE OIL

1 POUND GROUND BEEF

2 GARLIC CLOVES, MINCED

1 RED BELL PEPPER, DICED

3 CUPS SLICED FRESH MUSHROOMS (ABOUT 10
    OUNCES)

12 OUNCES CHEDDAR CHEESE, GRATED

1 CUP CORN KERNELS

ONE 10-OUNCE CAN CONDENSED TOMATO SOUP

1/2 CUP LIGHT CREAM

1 POUND DRIED MACARONI, SUCH AS ZITI OR
    FUSILLI

RED PEPPER FLAKES

SALT AND PEPPER

1.  Sauté the onion in the olive oil in a very large skillet over medium heat until softened, about 4 minutes. Add the beef and garlic and continue cooking until the beef is browned, about 5 minutes. Add the bell pepper and mushrooms and cook until softened, about 4 minutes. Add the Cheddar, corn, and tomato soup and simmer until the Cheddar is melted. Remove the pan from the heat and stir in the cream.

2.  Meanwhile, in a large pot of boiling salted water, cook the macaroni according to package directions until al dente. Drain.

3.  Serve the macaroni with the sauce poured over the top. Season to taste with red pepper flakes and salt and pepper.

---

*I pictured the army different. I pictured a lot of doughnuts and USO dances.*

—MATTHEW BRODERICK, *BILOXI BLUES*, 1988

During World War II, the Academy made the Oscars out of plaster instead of bronze, as a symbolic gesture of support for the war. After the war, the Academy replaced the winners' plaster Oscars with more permanent metal ones.

# MAPLE-GLAZED ANGEL FOOD CAKE

SERVES 12

*How extravagant you are, throwing away women like that.*

*Someday they may be scarce.*

CLAUDE RAINS, *CASABLANCA*, 1942

☆　☆　☆

Sugar was rationed during World War II, so a homemaker had to be creative to satisfy her family's sweet tooth, using sugar substitutes for baking, such as the syrup in canned fruit. This rich angel food cake, sweetened with wholesome, flavorful maple syrup, is from the World War II cookbook *300 Sugar Saving Recipes* by Harriet Hester. I've added my own non-wartime icing made with confectioner's sugar. Delicious, and fat-free to boot.

10 LARGE EGG WHITES

½ TEASPOON SALT

1 TEASPOON CREAM OF TARTAR

1 CUP CAKE FLOUR

1 CUP PLUS 3 TABLESPOONS PURE MAPLE SYRUP

1 TEASPOON VANILLA EXTRACT

1 CUP CONFECTIONERS' SUGAR

1. Preheat the oven to 350 degrees.

2. In a large mixing bowl, using an electric mixer set on high, beat the egg whites, salt, and cream of tartar until the egg whites form soft peaks, about 5 minutes. Reduce the mixer speed to medium and slowly add the flour, alternating with the 1 cup maple syrup, until just combined. Blend in the vanilla extract.

3. Pour the batter into an ungreased 9-inch tube pan and bake for about 35 minutes, or until golden.

4. Carefully invert the pan onto a wire rack and allow the cake to cool upside down in the pan, to prevent it from collapsing.

5. To make the glaze, whisk together the confectioners' sugar and the 3 tablespoons maple syrup until very smooth. Run a knife around the edges of the tube pan to remove the cake. Place the cooled cake on a serving platter and drizzle with the glaze.

# PEPPERMINT DEVIL'S FOOD SQUARES

SERVES 8

☆　☆　☆

This soft, moist, yet eggless cake, studded with pretty bits of red-and-white peppermint pieces, is as gorgeous as it is delicious. A great use for all those leftover Christmas candy canes!

4 TABLESPOONS (½ STICK) UNSALTED BUTTER, SOFTENED

½ CUP SUGAR

½ CUP BUTTERMILK

½ TEASPOON VANILLA EXTRACT

1 CUP CAKE FLOUR

½ CUP UNSWEETENED COCOA POWDER

½ TEASPOON BAKING SODA

½ TEASPOON SALT

1 CANDY CANE OR 6 PEPPERMINT CANDIES, FINELY CRUSHED

1. Preheat the oven to 375 degrees. Butter and flour an 8-inch square pan and set aside.

2. In a large bowl, using an electric mixer set on high, cream the butter and sugar together until fluffy, 2 to 3 minutes. Blend in the buttermilk and vanilla extract and then add the flour, cocoa powder, baking soda, and salt, mixing until just combined. The batter will be very stiff. Spread the batter out evenly in the prepared pan. Sprinkle the crushed candy on top and bake for 25 to 30 minutes, until a toothpick inserted in the center comes out clean. Transfer to a wire rack and allow to cool completely in the pan.

3. Cut into squares and serve.

Liquor sales soared during World War II. Liquor shortages were due not only to high consumer consumption, but also to the fact that alcohol was needed for the synthetic rubber in tires for military vehicles. Winemakers met the increased demand for alcoholic beverages by growing inexpensive higher-yielding grapes and producing lower-priced wines.

# JAM TRIANGLES

SERVES 12

*It's like finding a needle in a stack of needles.*
TOM HANKS, *SAVING PRIVATE RYAN*, 1998

☆   ☆   ☆

During World War II, bakers often used naturally sweetened jams and jellies in place of hard-to-find sugar. These yummy triangles can be filled with your favorite flavor of jam and are a great dessert or brunch treat.

6 TABLESPOONS (¾ STICK) UNSALTED BUTTER, SOFTENED

½ CUP COTTAGE CHEESE

1 CUP ALL-PURPOSE FLOUR

¼ CUP JAM

1 LARGE EGG, BEATEN

COARSE SUGAR, SUCH AS TURBINADO

1. In a bowl, using an electric mixer set on high, blend the butter and cottage cheese together until smooth. Reduce the mixer speed and slowly blend in the flour. Turn the dough out onto a piece of plastic wrap or waxed paper and flatten it into a disk. Wrap the dough tightly and refrigerate for about 30 minutes, or until firm.

2. Preheat the oven to 425 degrees. Line a baking sheet with parchment paper and set aside.

3. On a lightly floured work surface, roll the dough out into a 9-by-12-inch rectangle. Cut the dough into 3-inch squares. Put a level teaspoonful of the jam in the center of each square. Working with 1 square at a time, lightly brush the outer edges with the beaten egg. Fold 1 corner of the square over the jam to form a triangle. Press the edges to seal, and crimp the outer edges with a fork. Brush the tops of the triangles with the beaten egg and sprinkle generously with sugar. Bake the triangles for 15 minutes, or until golden brown. Allow to cool slightly before serving.

*He better be worth it. He better go home and cure a disease, or invent a longer-lasting lightbulb.*
—TOM HANKS, *SAVING PRIVATE RYAN*, 1998

The principal actors in *Saving Private Ryan* had to attend a special boot camp, a strenuous ten-day training program run by an ex-Marine. The actors—all except Matt Damon, who was purposely left out to encourage the other actors' resentment of him—slept in tents, ate army rations, and hiked five miles a day wearing forty-pound packs.

# COMFORT FOODS POTLUCK SUPPER

During World War II, "progressive parties" were extremely popular. No, not a political group—a progressive party was a get-together in which guests went from one home to another for each course. The World War II progressive-party idea inspired me to host a Veteran's Day potluck supper featuring comfort foods.

I have to admit right at the start that prior to this I had never hosted a potluck. I just couldn't imagine ever calling someone and saying, "Can you come over for dinner on Saturday? Great, bring the dinner." I didn't like being invited to potlucks, either. You know how some people have a recurring nightmare of showing up at school or for an important meeting with no clothes on? Well, my recurring nightmare is that I'm the only one whose food isn't eaten at a potluck. I'm always anxious about what to bring, and being anxious while you're cooking is a sure way to flub the food.

Then there is the issue of the menu mix. There always seems to be too much macaroni salad, including mine, and never enough fried chicken. The menu is usually all over the place, too. While I like an eclectic mix of foods, I just can't see pasta with clam sauce and corned beef and cabbage living together happily on one table.

For my potluck supper, I decided to be very specific about the dishes each guest should bring. Some might call it a tad controlling, but I gave everyone a written recipe. This actually solved two problems: Not only did the menu have a cohesive mix of foods, but I got to test all the recipes for this chapter, too!

It turned out that our friends loved being given recipes to follow because it took the pressure off contributing to the meal. Who knew? I was worried about being too bossy, but instead they appreciated the structure. A great lesson for your next potluck when you are dying to try out recipes from that new cookbook you just bought.

Besides the dishes in this chapter, I added other World War II classics such as SPAM, which soldiers called "ham that didn't pass the physical," and a platter of lima beans. Despite it being a "Victory Food Feature" and on special every week in every supermarket in America during the entire war, there was never, ever—not even once—a lima bean shortage!

Along with dessert, I put out bowls of M&M's, a candy invented during the war, and a box of assorted chocolates, so everyone, all together, could quote Forrest Gump: "Mama always said life was like a box of chocolates—you never know what you're gonna get."

The following is a list of some war-film classics to enjoy with your own comfort foods potluck supper.

## Movie Suggestions

*Above and Beyond,* 1952. Robert Taylor stars in story about the bombing of Hiroshima.

*Across the Pacific,* 1942. Humphrey Bogart war classic.

*Air Force,* 1943. World War II movie classic about fighter pilots.

*All Quiet on the Western Front,* 1930. Classic antiwar film. Remade as a TV movie in 1979.

*All the Young Men,* 1960. Sidney Poitier and Alan Ladd star in this movie about the Korean conflict.

*All Through the Night,* 1942. Story of Nazi spies in New York City, starring Humphrey Bogart and Peter Lorre.

*Anchors Aweigh,* 1945. Navy musical with Frank Sinatra and Gene Kelly.

*Apocalypse Now,* 1979. Vietnam War classic directed by Francis Ford Coppola, starring Marlon Brando.

*Biloxi Blues,* 1988. Neil Simon story. Stars Matthew Broderick as a boot camp recruit led by a colorful drill sergeant, played by Christopher Walken.

*Black Hawk Down,* 2001. Story of helicopter pilots shot down in 1993 over Somalia, directed by Ridley Scott.

*Born on the Fourth of July,* 1989. Stars Tom Cruise as a paralyzed Vietnam vet.

*The Bridge on the River Kwai,* 1957. Academy Award–winning movie starring William Holden and Alec Guinness.

*The Caine Mutiny,* 1954. Based on Herman Wouk's Pulitzer Prize–winning novel about a naval mutiny. Stars Humphrey Bogart, José Ferrer, and Lee Marvin.

*Casualties of War,* 1989. Sean Penn and Michael J. Fox star in the story of a Vietnamese woman killed by American soldiers.

*Catch-22,* 1970. Based on Joseph Heller's bestseller. Stars Alan Arkin.

*Caught in the Draft,* 1941. Bob Hope plays a movie star trying to dodge the draft. Must-see classic comedy.

*Coming Home,* 1978. Story of disabled Vietnam vets.

*The Dawn Patrol,* 1938. World War I classic starring Errol Flynn.

*The Deer Hunter,* 1978. Stars Robert De Niro and Christopher Walken.

*The Desert Fox,* 1951. Story of Rommel's defeat in Africa.

*The Diary of Anne Frank,* 1959. Based on the writings of a thirteen-year-old killed in a concentration camp in World War II.

*The Dirty Dozen,* 1967. Convicts are recruited to battle Nazis. Stars Lee Marvin, Ernest Borgnine, and Charles Bronson.

*The Eagle Has Landed,* 1976. World War II spy thriller starring Robert Duvall as a Nazi soldier.

*Flying Leathernecks,* 1951. Classic World War II film starring John Wayne.

*Flying Tigers,* 1942. Another classic war film starring John Wayne.

*From Here to Eternity,* 1953. Movie about a Hawaiian army base just before the attack on Pearl Harbor. Has the famous beach kissing scene. Stars Burt Lancaster, Montgomery Clift, and Deborah Kerr.

*Gallipoli,* 1981. Mel Gibson and Mark Lee star in the award-winning story of the Australian and Turkish World War I conflict.

*Good Morning, Vietnam,* 1987. Stars Robin Williams as a disc jockey.

*The Guns of Navarone,* 1961. World War II story of men sent to destroy weapons on the Greek island of Navarone. Star-studded cast includes Gregory Peck, Anthony Quinn, David Niven, and Richard Harris.

*Hot Shots!,* 1991. Fighter-pilot spoof starring Charlie Sheen.

*The Hunt for Red October,* 1990. Cold War story based on Tom Clancy's bestseller, starring Sean Connery.

*I Was a Male War Bride,* 1949. Cary Grant stars in this World War II comedy.

*Julia,* 1977. Meryl Streep's film debut. Story of a woman who smuggles money into Nazi territory to help a friend. Stars Jane Fonda and Vanessa Redgrave.

*Life Is Beautiful,* 1998. Roberto Benigni's stunning Holocaust story of a father's love.

*The Longest Day,* 1962. D-day epic starring John Wayne, Richard Burton, and Robert Mitchum.

*M\*A\*S\*H,* 1970. Antiwar comedy about a medical unit in Korea, starring Donald Sutherland, Elliott Gould, and Sally Kellerman.

*Mister Roberts,* 1955. Story of a prank-playing navy cargo crew, starring Henry Fonda, James Cagney, and Jack Lemmon.

*Patton,* 1970. Epic starring George C. Scott as General George S. Patton Jr.

*Pearl Harbor,* 2001. Stars Ben Affleck and Alec Baldwin.

*Platoon,* 1986. Vivid depiction of the Vietnam War, starring Willem Dafoe and Charlie Sheen.

*Sands of Iwo Jima,* 1949. Must-see for John Wayne fans.

*Saving Private Ryan,* 1998. Spielberg epic about the military's attempt to save one soldier. Stars Tom Hanks and Matt Damon.

*Schindler's List,* 1993. Oscar-winning film by Steven Spielberg about a German businessman who bribes Nazis to keep Jews out of concentration camps.

*Stalag 17,* 1953. A classic film about Americans in a German POW camp. Stars William Holden and Otto Preminger.

*Wake Island,* 1942. One of the most popular films during World War II. Stars Robert Preston.

*What Price Glory?,* 1952. Comedy set in World War II France, starring James Cagney.

*Where Eagles Dare,* 1968. Action-packed World War II adventure starring Clint Eastwood and Richard Burton.

# GANGSTERS TO GREASERS

### COMING ATTRACTIONS
THREE *P*'S SALAD ★ FROSTED SANDWICH ★ PROHIBITION PUNCH

### FEATURE PRESENTATION
SPAGHETTI AND MEATBALLS WITH EGGPLANT ★ DUNCAN HINES STROGANOFF
ICEBERG WEDGES WITH BLUE CHEESE DRESSING ★ THE ORIGINAL CAESAR SALAD

### CLOSING CREDITS
ICEBOX CAKE ★ MYSTERY CAKE ★ MOCK APPLE PIE

### LIGHTS, CAMERA, ACTION! SPEAKEASY PARTY
MOVIE SUGGESTIONS

This chapter touches on the food and dining influences of the Roaring Twenties, the Depression, and the 1950s. Each time period sparked its own distinctive foods and films.

The 1920s, the Jazz Age, as it was called, was a decade marked by Prohibition, bootleggers, and gangsters, inspiring such films as *Chicago, Angels with Dirty Faces, The Untouchables,* and *The Godfather.* Sid Grauman first opened his famed Grauman's Chinese Theatre then and began the tradition of actors leaving footprints in the cement out front. Stars of the decade included matinee idol Rudolph Valentino, as well as Charlie Chaplin, Greta Garbo, and Douglas Fairbanks Jr.

The stock market crash on October 24, 1929, marked the end of the Roaring Twenties and the start of the Depression. Theater attendance soared during the Depression, fueled by people hungry for a laugh, a little glamour, and a distraction from the hard times. Some of the funniest and best Hollywood films were made in the thirties, starring actors such as Clark Gable, Errol Flynn, Greta Garbo, Jean Harlow, Gary Cooper, W. C. Fields, Mae West, Laurel and Hardy, and the Marx Brothers.

Prohibition was repealed on December 5, 1933, and with its end came the advent of the cocktail party and the birth of the martini, "a medium-dry Martini, lemon peel, shaken not stirred" (*Dr. No,* 1962). Bite-sized nibbles, tailor-made for eating while holding a drink, were all the rage, and in 1940 legendary chef James Beard wrote America's first cookbook on hors d'oeuvres.

After the Depression and World War II, America entered into a period of relative calm and prosperity. The 1950s, a decade of bobby socks, poodle skirts, and leather jackets, so well depicted in the hit movie *Grease,* ushered in the American suburban era. With the suburbs came backyard barbecues and outdoor grilling.

Enjoy rediscovering the food fads of America's colorful past in these easy-to-prepare and delicious recipes from cookbooks and ladies' magazines of the time.

# THREE *P*'S SALAD

SERVES 6

*It's the face powder that gets a man interested,*
*but it's the baking powder that keeps him home.*
GENE HACKMAN, *BONNIE AND CLYDE*, 1967

☆ ☆ ☆

Betty Crocker was never a real person. "Born" in 1921, Betty Crocker was at first only a signature and a voice on a radio program created to answer consumer questions about Gold Medal flour. She didn't have a face until a portrait was commissioned in the mid-1930s. Betty Crocker represented one twenties ideal, the perfect happy homemaker, while the flapper represented the decade's "other woman."

Sweet pickles, a twenties favorite food, was mixed with peas and peanuts to create an unusual Jazz Age salad well worth rediscovering.

½ CUP CHOPPED SWEET PICKLES
½ CUP COARSELY CHOPPED PEANUTS
½ CUP COOKED PEAS
2 TABLESPOONS MAYONNAISE
SALT AND PEPPER
6 OUTER LEAVES OF ICEBERG LETTUCE

1. Combine the pickles, peanuts, peas, and mayonnaise in a bowl. Season to taste with salt and pepper.

2. To serve, divide the salad evenly among the lettuce leaf "cups."

---

*Sweet Santa Claus, give me him!* —CLARA BOW, *IT*, 1927

Clara Bow, who often played a flapper, was called the "It" girl after her 1927 hit movie *It*. "It" was, of course, sex appeal. The flapper immortalized in the cartoon character Betty Boop is probably the best-known icon of the Jazz Age. Movies such as *Love 'Em and Leave 'Em, Rolled Stockings, Hula, Mantrap,* and *The Saturday Night Kid* are some of the films made at the time about those colorful young women.

# FROSTED SANDWICH

SERVES 2

*And then I started foolin' around . . . and then I started screwin' around,*
*which is foolin' around without dinner.*

RENÉE ZELLWEGER, *CHICAGO*, 2002

☆  ☆  ☆

Because of Prohibition, tearooms opened across America as a place to socialize, have a nibble and a quick drink . . . of tea, that is. Sandwiches were made of cream cheese and coated to look like small frosted cakes. These sandwiches are the cat's pajamas and the bee's knees.

3 THIN SLICES WHITE OR WHOLE WHEAT
   SANDWICH BREAD

2 TABLESPOONS BUTTER, SOFTENED

2 THIN SLICES DELI HAM

2 TO 3 THIN SLICES TOMATO

2 TEASPOONS CHOPPED DRAINED CAPERS

SALT AND PEPPER

2 OUNCES WHIPPED CREAM CHEESE

GARNISHES SUCH AS FRESH PARSLEY LEAVES,
   CHOPPED FRESH CHIVES, PAPRIKA, AND FRESH
   DILL SPRIGS (OPTIONAL)

1. Place the bread on a work surface and butter each slice. Lay the ham on 1 of the buttered slices and cover with another slice of bread, butter side down. Butter the top of that second slice and top with the tomato slices and capers. Season generously with salt and pepper. Add the last bread slice, butter side down. Gently press the sandwich to adhere the layers and, using a sharp knife, cut off the crusts. Transfer to a serving plate and "frost" the sandwich with the cream cheese. Decorate each corner of the sandwich with your favorite garnish, such as a fresh dill sprig or a sprinkle of paprika.

2. Cut the sandwich diagonally into 4 triangles and serve on 2 small plates with dessert forks and knifes.

---

*—You know, I was there. I was*
*there that night you plugged your husband.*
*—So was half of Chicago*

—RENÉE ZELLWEGER AND CATHERINE ZETA-JONES, *CHICAGO*, 2002

Nicole Kidman, Madonna, Britney Spears, Gwyneth Paltrow, and Cameron Diaz were all considered for the starring roles of Velma Kelly and Roxie Hart in *Chicago,* the Academy Award–winning movie based on the hit Broadway musical.

# PROHIBITION PUNCH

SERVES 8

*—They say they're going to repeal Prohibition. What will you do then?*

*—I think I'll have a drink.*

A REPORTER AND KEVIN COSTNER, *THE UNTOUCHABLES*, 1987

☆  ☆  ☆

Prohibition sparked an era of speakeasies, gin mills, and whoopee parlors that supplied bootleg whiskey. The harsh taste of this inferior liquor influenced the creation of sweet mixed drinks like the brandy Alexander, as well as a slew of nonalcoholic punches. This refreshing punch from a twenties ladies' magazine, made with mint jelly, was originally suggested as a nonalcoholic bridge-party beverage. Nonteetotalers should note, though, that it is fantastic with a generous splash of hooch.

1½ CUPS SUGAR

5 TEA BAGS

½ CUP MINT JELLY

1 CUP GRAPEFRUIT JUICE

1 CUP PINEAPPLE JUICE

JUICE OF 4 LEMONS

1. Bring 3 cups of water and the sugar to a boil in a small saucepan. Cook until the sugar is completely dissolved. Remove from the heat, add the tea bags, and allow to steep for 5 minutes. Remove the tea bags and discard. Stir the mint jelly into the hot tea until completely dissolved.

2. Pour the tea mixture into a large pitcher along with the grapefruit, pineapple, and lemon juices and refrigerate until cold. Serve over ice.

*People are going to drink. You know that, and I know that; we all know that. And all I do is act on that. And all this talk of bootlegging. What is bootlegging? On a boat it's bootlegging; on Lake Shore Drive it's hospitality.* —ROBERT DE NIRO, *THE UNTOUCHABLES*, 1987

Remember that scene where Eliot Ness confiscates what he thinks is Canadian whiskey only to be duped by Al Capone with crates of parasols? Well, several books on movie bloopers erroneously cite the use of a maple leaf on the cases as a mistake, claiming that the maple leaf wasn't a symbol of Canada in the twenties. While it is true that the red maple leaf wasn't used on the Canadian flag until the 1960s, the maple leaf has been a symbol adopted by Canada since at least the 1860s, when the Prince of Wales visited there.

# SPAGHETTI AND MEATBALLS WITH EGGPLANT

SERVES 6 ("THE FAMILY")

*Come over here, kid; learn something. You never know, you might
have to cook for twenty guys sometime. You see, you start out with a
little bit of oil and you fry some garlic, then you throw in some
tomatoes, tomato paste; you fry it. You make sure it doesn't stick. You
get it to a boil and you shove in all your sausages and meatballs.
Add a little bit of wine, a little bit of sugar . . .*

RICHARD S. CASTELLANO, *THE GODFATHER*, 1972

☆  ☆  ☆

Watching the *Godfather* movies always makes me hungry. There must be fifty food scenes in the first *Godfather* alone. Although I'm Italian American and have seen spaghetti and meatballs made all my life, I researched how it was done in America during the gangster years of the twenties and thirties. I cringe to repeat the awful things done to unsuspecting pasta back then. You'd probably rather swim with the fishes than eat what passed for twenties "Italian spaghetti"; one recipe even instructed unsuspecting Americans to bake pasta with ketchup.

This is my Sicilian grandmother's authentic Old World recipe. *Buòn appetito!*

**MEATBALLS**

5 SLICES WHITE SANDWICH BREAD, CRUSTS
 REMOVED

1 POUND GROUND BEEF

8 OUNCES GROUND PORK

2 LARGE EGGS

½ ONION, FINELY MINCED

3 TABLESPOONS GRATED PARMESAN CHEESE

3 TABLESPOONS FINELY MINCED FRESH PARSLEY

1 TEASPOON FENNEL SEED, SLIGHTLY CRUSHED

¼ TEASPOON FRESHLY GRATED NUTMEG

¼ TEASPOON SALT

¼ TEASPOON PEPPER

1 TABLESPOON EXTRA-VIRGIN OLIVE OIL

1. Tear the bread into small pieces and place in a large bowl. Sprinkle with a few tablespoons of water and allow to stand for a few minutes, until the water is absorbed. Squeeze out any excess. Add the beef, pork, eggs, onion, Parmesan, parsley, fennel seed, nutmeg, salt, and pepper and mix until just combined.

2. Form meatballs, about 2 inches in diameter (you should get about 13). Heat the olive oil in a large nonstick skillet over medium-high heat. Add the meatballs and brown on all sides, turning as necessary, about 3 minutes per side. Reserve.

**SAUCE AND EGGPLANT**

¼ CUP EXTRA-VIRGIN OLIVE OIL, PLUS MORE AS
    NEEDED

1 LARGE ONION, MINCED

4 GARLIC CLOVES, MINCED

ONE 28-OUNCE CAN CRUSHED TOMATOES

½ CUP RED WINE

1½ TABLESPOONS SUGAR

2 TABLESPOONS FRESH PARSLEY

1 TEASPOON FENNEL SEED, SLIGHTLY CRUSHED

1 BAY LEAF

SALT AND PEPPER

1 LARGE EGGPLANT

1 POUND SPAGHETTI

12 LARGE FRESH BASIL LEAVES

1. In a large, heavy-bottomed pot, heat 2 tablespoons of the olive oil over medium-high heat. Add the onion and cook, stirring frequently, until golden, 5 to 6 minutes. Add the garlic and continue cooking until softened, about 1 minute. Stir in the tomatoes, wine, sugar, parsley, fennel seed, and bay leaf. Bring to a boil, then reduce the heat to maintain a simmer. Cook for 5 minutes, season to taste with salt and pepper, and then gently add the meatballs and the meatball pan juices, submerging the meatballs in the sauce. Cover and cook for 50 minutes.

2. Meanwhile, peel the eggplant and cut lengthwise into ¼-inch-thick slices. Then make 2 cuts from the bottom of the large end of each slice halfway up to make 3 sections yet keep the eggplant slice intact. Generously salt both sides of the eggplant slices and lay them in a single layer on a rack, or on paper towels, for 15 minutes. Pat well with paper towels to remove all the excess moisture. Heat the remaining 2 tablespoons olive oil in a large nonstick skillet over medium-high heat. Add the eggplant slices in 1 layer and fry, turning once, until dark golden, about 5 minutes per side. Transfer to a paper-towel-lined plate to drain. Repeat with the remaining eggplant, adding more oil as necessary.

3. Bring a large pot of salted water to a boil. Add the spaghetti and cook according to package directions. Drain.

4. To serve, remove the meatballs from the sauce and cover to keep warm. Discard the bay leaf. Put the spaghetti into a large bowl and pour the sauce over it, tossing well to coat. Divide the pasta among 6 plates. Top with a slice of fried eggplant and lay a basil leaf or two over the top. Serve warm.

5. Serve the meatballs after the pasta course with a green salad and crusty bread.

---

*I'm gonna make him an offer he can't refuse.* —MARLON BRANDO, *THE GODFATHER*, 1972

Marlon Brando refused the offer to appear in *The Godfather: Part II,* which nevertheless went on to make film history as the only sequel ever to win the Academy Award for Best Picture.

# DUNCAN HINES STROGANOFF

SERVES 6

*I grew up in a tough neighborhood, and we used to say,*
*"You can get further with a kind word and a gun than just a kind word."*

ROBERT DE NIRO, *THE UNTOUCHABLES*, 1987

☆　☆　☆

Duncan Hines, who later became associated with cake mixes, was originally a traveling salesman who became famous for his guide to restaurants called *Adventures in Good Eating.* This recipe for creamy stroganoff, which became a fifties staple, comes from his cookbook, *Adventures in Good Cooking,* the best recipes from his favorite eating spots across America.

Duncan Hines suggests serving stroganoff with rice, melba toast, or rye bread. However, I like buttered egg noodles best.

| | |
|---|---|
| 2 POUNDS ROUND STEAK, CUT INTO 1-INCH CUBES | 1 LARGE ONION, MINCED |
| SALT AND PEPPER | 1 CUP SOUR CREAM |
| ALL-PURPOSE FLOUR | 1½ TABLESPOONS CIDER VINEGAR |
| 2 TABLESPOONS OLIVE OIL | 1 TEASPOON WORCESTERSHIRE SAUCE |
| 2 TABLESPOONS BUTTER | 1 TEASPOON DIJON MUSTARD |
| 3 CUPS SLICED FRESH MUSHROOMS, ABOUT 10 OUNCES | 3 TABLESPOONS CHOPPED FRESH PARSLEY |
| | BUTTERED EGG NOODLES |

1. Generously season the steak with salt and pepper. In a large bowl, toss the meat cubes with flour until well coated, shaking off the excess. Heat 1 tablespoon of the olive oil in a large, deep skillet over high heat. Add the steak and sear until browned on all sides, about 5 minutes. Transfer the meat and any liquids it expelled to a bowl and reserve.

2. Melt the butter and the remaining 1 tablespoon olive oil in the same skillet over medium heat. Add the mushrooms and onion and cook until softened, about 5 minutes. Add the steak and juices and the sour cream, stirring until well combined. Reduce the heat to medium-low, cover, and cook until the sauce thickens, about 30 minutes. Stir in the vinegar, Worcestershire sauce, Dijon mustard, and salt and pepper to taste. Top with the parsley.

3. Serve hot over buttered egg noodles.

*Sandy, you can't just walk out of a drive-in.* —JOHN TRAVOLTA, *GREASE,* 1978

John Travolta, star of the movie *Grease,* had years before played Doody in the live theatrical production of the musical.

Olivia Newton-John's zipper broke and she had to be sewn into the black slacks she wore for her last big number in the film. Terrified that she might have to go to the rest room, the star didn't drink anything for the entire scene.

Some classic exchanges in *Grease* include:

*—Oh, bite the weenie, Riz.*
*—With relish.*

and

*—That is so adolescent.*
*—We are adolescent.*

I also liked the one-liners "I feel like a defective typewriter. . . . I skipped a period" and "If you can't be an athlete, be an athletic supporter."

# ICEBERG WEDGES WITH BLUE CHEESE DRESSING

SERVES 4

*Look at that! Look how she moves! That's just like Jell-O on springs.*

JACK LEMMON, *SOME LIKE IT HOT*, 1959

☆  ☆  ☆

Gelatin salads were all the rage from the turn of the century until well into the sixties. These salads were made in molds with ingredients that varied from grated carrots and pineapple in lemon-flavored gelatin to Perfection Salad, a combination of cabbage, celery, and red bell peppers suspended in lemon-and-vinegar-flavored gelatin.

I tried dozens and dozens of these old recipes, hoping to include one in this chapter. However, although many were very pretty, I could not hit on any recipe that the taste-testers or my family would eat. Here instead is a sure-to-please-everyone salad, a classic from the 1930s cookbook *The Joy of Cooking* by Irma Rombauer.

¼ CUP SOUR CREAM

¼ CUP HEAVY CREAM

½ TEASPOON WORCESTERSHIRE SAUCE

½ TEASPOON RED WINE VINEGAR

¼ TEASPOON SALT

⅛ TEASPOON DRY MUSTARD

PINCH OF PEPPER

2 OUNCES BLUE CHEESE, CRUMBLED

1 LARGE HEAD ICEBERG LETTUCE

1. In a bowl, whisk together the sour cream, heavy cream, Worcestershire sauce, vinegar, salt, mustard, and pepper until smooth. Stir in the blue cheese until combined. Cover and refrigerate until ready to use.

2. To serve, cut the lettuce into quarters and divide among 4 plates. Pour the dressing across the top of each iceberg wedge.

---

—*You ain't got money for dinner, let alone for buying a car.*

—*Well, I'll tell you, I got enough money for a Coca-Cola.*

—FAYE DUNAWAY AND WARREN BEATTY, *BONNIE AND CLYDE*, 1967

Coca-Cola, originally sold as a "nerve and brain tonic," was remarketed as tasty syrup for seltzer in the 1880s and bottled in 1894. Named after the early cocaine-containing ingredients, the coca leaf and the kola nut, any traces of the stimulant were removed from the formula by 1929. During Prohibition, sales of soft drinks like Coke soared.

# THE ORIGINAL CAESAR SALAD

*All right, Mr. DeMille, I'm ready for my close-up.*

GLORIA SWANSON, *SUNSET BOULEVARD*, 1950

☆　☆　☆

Hollywood celebrities like Cecil B. DeMille traveled south of the border for food and drink during Prohibition. An Italian restaurant owner in Tijuana who catered to these stars is credited with inventing the Caesar salad. The original, which didn't have anchovies, was concocted from whatever was on hand.

SIX ¼-INCH-THICK SLICES BAGUETTE

½ CUP OLIVE OIL

2 LARGE GARLIC CLOVES, MINCED

SALT

JUICE OF 1 LEMON

¾ CUP GRATED PARMESAN CHEESE

2 TEASPOONS SUGAR

PEPPER

1 LARGE HEAD ROMAINE LETTUCE, TORN INTO 2-INCH PIECES

1 TABLESPOON CAPERS, DRAINED

1. Preheat the broiler.

2. Lay the baguette slices on an ungreased baking sheet. In a measuring cup, stir together the olive oil and garlic. Using a pastry brush, lightly brush both sides of the baguette slices with the garlic oil. Season the bread with salt and broil, turning once, for about 2 minutes per side, or until golden brown. Allow to cool, then coarsely crumble. Set aside.

3. In a very large bowl, stir together the lemon juice, Parmesan, and sugar until well mixed. Whisk in the remaining garlic oil until well combined. Season to taste with salt and pepper. Add the lettuce to the bowl and toss lightly to coat.

4. To serve, divide among 6 plates and top with the crumbled toasted baguette and the capers.

---

*This is Hollywood, land of dreams. Some dreams come true, some don't, but keep on dreamin'. This is Hollywood.* —ABDUL SALAAM EL RAZZAC, *PRETTY WOMAN*, 1990

The wife of the real estate owner who developed Hollywood gave it its name. The wife had heard a woman talking on a train about her estate called "Holly Wood," liked the way it sounded, and suggested the name to her husband.

# ICEBOX CAKE

SERVES 8

*This is terrific! I either have a monster in my refrigerator*

*or I'm completely crazy.*

SIGOURNEY WEAVER, *GHOSTBUSTERS*, 1984

☆  ☆  ☆

Once refrigerators became available in the 1920s, a crop of icebox recipes became popular so owners could show off their new purchases. This delicious no-bake dessert is so easy, they joked back then that even a flapper could make it.

2 CUPS MILK

2 TABLESPOONS BUTTER

2 TABLESPOONS SUGAR

$2\frac{1}{2}$ TABLESPOONS CORNSTARCH

4 OUNCES SEMISWEET CHOCOLATE, FINELY CHOPPED

1 TEASPOON VANILLA EXTRACT

36 LADYFINGERS

WHIPPED CREAM

1. Heat $1\frac{1}{2}$ cups of the milk, the butter, and the sugar in a saucepan over medium-low heat until hot but not boiling. Dissolve the cornstarch in the remaining $\frac{1}{2}$ cup milk and set aside. While stirring continuously, add the chocolate to the saucepan and stir until smooth, about 5 minutes. When the mixture begins to simmer, slowly stir in the milk-cornstarch mixture. Bring to a simmer while stirring and cook until very thick, about 2 minutes. Remove from the heat and stir in the vanilla extract.

2. Arrange 18 of the ladyfingers in 1 layer in the bottom of an 8-inch-square baking dish. Spread half of the chocolate pudding evenly over the ladyfingers. Top with the remaining 18 ladyfingers, in 1 layer, then spread evenly with the rest of the pudding. Cover with plastic wrap, allowing the plastic to touch the entire surface to prevent a skin from forming. Refrigerate for at least 2 hours before serving.

3. To serve, cut into squares and top with whipped cream.

*Smoke gets in your eyes.*

—IRENE DUNNE, *ROBERTA*, 1935

Composer Jerome Kern, who wrote hits for movies such as *Show Boat, Cover Girl,* and *Swing Time,* contributed a recipe to a Prohibition-era cookbook. The recipe included the ingredient Kern called "pre-Prohibition sherry" and explained that if none was available, "the names and addresses of seventy-one bootleggers can be supplied." Kern ended the detailed recipe with the advice to forget about the food and just serve the sherry.

# MYSTERY CAKE

SERVES 12

*—Well, that's you in a nutshell.*

*—No, this is me in a nutshell: "Help! I'm in a nutshell. . . ."*

ELIZABETH HURLEY AND MIKE MYERS, *AUSTIN POWERS: INTERNATIONAL MAN OF MYSTERY*, 1997

☆　☆　☆

This recipe, from a 1933 issue of *American Cookery Magazine,* has a mystery ingredient—a can of condensed tomato soup! No one will be able to guess the mystery ingredient in this spicy, rich fruit and nut cake.

8 TABLESPOONS (1 STICK) UNSALTED BUTTER, SOFTENED

1 CUP GRANULATED SUGAR

3 LARGE EGGS, AT ROOM TEMPERATURE

ONE 10-OUNCE CAN CONDENSED TOMATO SOUP

2 TEASPOONS BAKING POWDER

1 TEASPOON BAKING SODA

1 TEASPOON GROUND CINNAMON

½ TEASPOON GROUND CLOVES

½ TEASPOON GROUND ALLSPICE

½ TEASPOON GROUND NUTMEG

¼ TEASPOON SALT

3 CUPS CAKE FLOUR

½ CUP CHOPPED PITTED DATES

½ CUP CHOPPED DRIED APRICOTS

¼ CUP CHOPPED WALNUTS

CONFECTIONERS' SUGAR

1. Preheat the oven to 350 degrees.

2. Butter and lightly flour a 12-cup Bundt pan and set aside.

3. In a large bowl, using an electric mixer set on high, blend the butter and granulated sugar together until light and fluffy, about 5 minutes. Add the eggs, one at a time, mixing well after each addition. Add the condensed tomato soup, baking powder, baking soda, cinnamon, cloves, allspice, nutmeg, and salt and mix until well combined. Reduce the mixer speed to low and add the flour in 3 batches, mixing after each addition until just combined. Stir in the dried fruit and the walnuts and pour into the prepared pan, spreading evenly.

4. Bake for 40 minutes, or until a toothpick inserted in the center comes out clean.

5. Allow the cake to cool in the pan on a rack for 10 minutes, then invert onto the rack and allow to cool completely before serving.

6. When cool, dust with confectioners' sugar.

> *I don't like the way you're walking. You've been into the sacramental wine again.*
>
> —MEL BROOKS, *BLAZING SADDLES*, 1974
>
> During Prohibition, priests and rabbis were allowed to transport wine for religious services. During Prohibition, there was a mysterious rise in applications for the ministry!

# MOCK APPLE PIE

SERVES 8

*Come along, Dorothy. You don't want any of those apples.*

RAY BOLGER, *THE WIZARD OF OZ,* 1939

☆ ☆ ☆

This recipe, popular during the Depression, when crackers were free but an apple cost a penny, is from a thirties box of Ritz. Moist and buttery, this pie will have you convinced you're eating the real thing.

1 READY-MADE 9-INCH DOUBLE PIECRUST

36 BUTTER CRACKERS, COARSELY CRUSHED

2 CUPS SUGAR

2 TEASPOONS CREAM OF TARTAR

GRATED ZEST OF 1 LEMON

2 TABLESPOONS FRESHLY SQUEEZED LEMON JUICE

½ TEASPOON GROUND CINNAMON

¼ TEASPOON GROUND NUTMEG OR ALLSPICE

2 TABLESPOONS UNSALTED BUTTER, DICED

1. Preheat the oven to 425 degrees.

2. Fill the bottom crust with the crushed crackers. In a saucepan, bring the sugar, cream of tartar, and 1½ cups of water to a boil. Reduce the heat to maintain a low boil and cook for 15 minutes. Remove from the heat and stir in the lemon zest, lemon juice, cinnamon, and nutmeg.

3. Pour the mixture over the crackers and dot with the butter. Cover the pie with the upper crust and crimp the top and bottom edges together.

4. Bake for 35 minutes, or until golden. Allow the pie to cool for 20 minutes, or until the liquid has been absorbed, before serving.

---

*One day the kids from the neighborhood carried my mother's groceries all the way home.*
*You know why? It was outta respect.* —RAY LIOTTA, *GOODFELLAS,* 1990

In *Goodfellas,* a movie about "the family," director Martin Scorsese cast his own mother to play Joe Pesci's mom in the film.

# SPEAKEASY PARTY

*As far back as I can remember, I always wanted to be a gangster.*

—RAY LIOTTA, *GOODFELLAS*, 1990

A speakeasy-themed party is great fun because of the wonderful costume, prop, drink, and food possibilities. Guests can come as Roaring Twenties flappers, gangsters in suits, or black-leather greasers.

Give everyone a password on their invitation and fill your bathtub with ice and bottles of gin to set the scene. Be sure to serve a pitcher of brandy Alexander—the drink invented during Prohibition—as well as a nonalcoholic punch for teetotalers. Near the punch bowl, as a reminder of the fads of the era like flagpole sitting, mah-jongg, dance marathons, and live-goldfish swallowing, you might like to put out a large glass bowl filled with Goldfish crackers or set up a mah-jongg game.

With dinner, you might like to play jazz classics by Louis Armstrong, Ethel Waters, and Bill Robinson or some hit songs of the era, such as "Yes, We Have No Bananas," "Ain't We Got Fun," "Makin' Whoopee," and "Second Hand Rose."

Below is a list of gangster and greaser classics to enjoy at your speakeasy party.

# Movie Suggestions

*All the King's Men,* 1949. Movie based on the life of corrupt Depression-era politician Huey Long.

*Analyze This,* 1999. Comedy about a Mob boss, played by Robert De Niro, who sees a psychologist, Billy Crystal.

*Angels with Dirty Faces,* 1938. Must-see classic James Cagney gangster movie.

*Atlantic City,* 1980. Burt Lancaster plays an aging mobster.

*Back to the Future,* 1985. Teenager is transported back to his parents' fifties high school.

*Bonnie and Clyde,* 1967. Based on the true story of 1930s criminals Bonnie Parker and Clyde Barrow. Stars Warren Beatty and Faye Dunaway.

*Bound for Glory,* 1976. Based on the life of folk singer Woody Guthrie during the Depression era.

*Bugsy,* 1991. Story of gangster Bugsy Siegel, who built Las Vegas. Stars Warren Beatty and Annette Bening.

*Bullets Over Broadway,* 1994. Woody Allen spoof of gangsters in the Jazz Age. Stars Dianne Wiest, John Cusack, and Chazz Palminteri.

*Bye Bye Birdie,* 1963. Musical about a fifties teen idol who is drafted. Stars Ann-Margret.

*Casino,* 1995. Must-see Scorsese film about Las Vegas and the Mob. Stars Sharon Stone and Robert De Niro.

*Chicago,* 2002. Musical about Roaring Twenties female criminals, starring Renée Zellweger, Catherine Zeta-Jones, and Richard Gere.

*The Cotton Club,* 1984. Gregory Hines, Nicolas Cage, and Richard Gere star in this gangster musical by Francis Ford Coppola.

*Dick Tracy,* 1990. Movie based on the 1930s comic strip, produced and directed by, and starring, Warren Beatty. Also stars Madonna, Al Pacino, James Caan, and Dustin Hoffman.

*Dillinger,* 1973. Based on the life of Depression-era bank robber John Dillinger. Stars Richard Dreyfuss.

*Diner,* 1982. A bleak look at the fifties. Stars Kevin Bacon and Ellen Barkin.

*Force of Evil,* 1948. Film-noir Mafia classic.

*The Funeral,* 1996. Story of thirties gangsters. Stars Christopher Walken.

*The Godfather,* 1972. Mafia classic by Francis Ford Coppola. Followed by the must-see sequels, *The Godfather: Part II* and *Part III.*

*Goodfellas,* 1990. Classic film about "wise guys," starring Joe Pesci, Ray Liotta, Robert De Niro, and Debi Mazar.

*The Grapes of Wrath,* 1940. Movie based on John Steinbeck's novel about the Depression. Stars Henry Fonda.

*Grease,* 1978. Must-see musical set in the fifties, starring John Travolta and Olivia Newton-John.

*The Great Gatsby,* 1974. Based on F. Scott Fitzgerald's novel, set in the twenties. Stars Mia Farrow and Robert Redford.

*Hard Times,* 1975. Story of a Depression-era street fighter, starring Charles Bronson and James Coburn.

*Ironweed,* 1987. Painfully moving account of the Depression. Stars Meryl Streep and Jack Nicholson.

*Last Exit to Brooklyn,* 1989. Mafia story set in the fifties.

*Mad Dog and Glory,* 1993. Robert De Niro plays a mild-mannered cop battling gangster Bill Murray.

*Mafia!,* 1998. Mob spoof starring Lloyd Bridges.

*Married to the Mob,* 1988. Mafia widow Michelle Pfeiffer tries to leave "the family."

*Mean Streets,* 1973. This Mafia movie, set in Little Italy, New York City, is director Martin Scorsese's debut. Stars Robert De Niro.

*Mickey Blue Eyes,* 1999. Mafia comedy starring Hugh Grant.

*Miller's Crossing,* 1990. Film mix of Italian, Irish, and Jewish gangsters, starring John Turturro and Albert Finney.

*Modern Times,* 1936. Charlie Chaplin classic about the Depression and the machine age.

*Once Upon a Time in America,* 1984. Story of the Mafia in the twenties. Stars Robert De Niro and James Woods.

*Of Mice and Men,* 1992. Movie set in the Depression era, based on John Steinbeck's novel. Stars John Malkovich. The 1939 version, starring Lon Chaney Jr. and Burgess Meredith, is also great.

*Paper Moon,* 1973. Story of con artists in the Depression, starring Ryan and Tatum O'Neal.

*Peggy Sue Got Married,* 1986. Kathleen Turner stars as a wife who is transported back to her fifties high school years.

*Pennies from Heaven*, 1981. Musical set during the Depression, starring Steve Martin and
  Bernadette Peters.

*Prizzi's Honor*, 1985. Black comedy about the Mob, starring Jack Nicholson, Kathleen Turner, and
  Anjelica Huston.

*Public Enemies*, 1996. Thirties crime spree by "Ma" Barker and her sons.

*The Public Enemy*, 1931. Stars James Cagney as a mobster. This is the movie with the famous
  grapefruit-in-the-face scene.

*Rebel Without a Cause*, 1955. James Dean classic about a troubled teenager. Also stars Natalie
  Wood and Sal Mineo.

*Scarface*, 1932. Movie based on the life of Al Capone. Stars George Raft and Boris Karloff.

*School Ties*, 1992. The McCarthy-era fifties portrayed in a high school football setting. Stars Brendan
  Fraser and Matt Damon.

*State of Grace*, 1990. Sean Penn and Ed Harris star in this cops-and-gangsters story.

*The Sting*, 1973. Paul Newman and Robert Redford star as Depression-era con artists. Must-see
  classic.

*They Shoot Horses, Don't They?*, 1969. Very moving story of Depression-era marathon dance
  contests. Stars Jane Fonda and Red Buttons.

*The Untouchables*, 1987. Must-see movie about crime boss Al Capone and federal agent Eliot Ness.
  Stars Kevin Costner and Robert De Niro.

*The Way We Were*, 1973. Romance between two star-crossed lovers that spans the thirties through
  the fifties, with Barbra Streisand and Robert Redford.

*White Heat*, 1949. Mob film that includes James Cagney's famous scene on top of a burning oil
  tanker.

# ROMANTIC DINNER FOR TWO

**COMING ATTRACTIONS**

SPAGHETTI ALLA PUTTANESCA ★ GINGER-CITRUS SHRIMP WITH SUGAR SNAP PEAS

**FEATURE PRESENTATION**

ASPARAGUS ITALIAN-STYLE ★ BEEF TENDERLOIN WITH PINK PEPPERCORN SAUCE

**INTERMISSION**

JUST A BITE: ROMAINE LEAVES WITH RADISH VINAIGRETTE

**CLOSING CREDITS**

TIRAMISÙ ★ INDIVIDUAL KAHLÚA CHOCOLATE CAKES ★ STRAWBERRIES WITH BALSAMIC VINEGAR

**LIGHTS, CAMERA, ACTION! CANDLELIT SUPPER**

MOVIE SUGGESTIONS

# SPAGHETTI ALLA PUTTANESCA

SERVES 2

*Oh, inhibitions are always nice, because they're so nice to overcome.*

JANE FONDA, *KLUTE*, 1971

☆　☆　☆

According to legend, Italian prostitutes invented this luscious spicy pasta dish as a quick meal between clients. Mira Sorvino in *Mighty Aphrodite* (1995), Elisabeth Shue in *Leaving Las Vegas* (1995), Jane Fonda in *Klute* (1971), Elizabeth Taylor in *Butterfield 8* (1960), and Shirley Jones in *Elmer Gantry* (1960) all won their Oscars portraying prostitutes.

⅓ POUND THIN SPAGHETTI

2 TABLESPOONS EXTRA-VIRGIN OLIVE OIL

2 TABLESPOONS MINCED RED ONION

2 GARLIC CLOVES, MINCED

¼ TEASPOON RED PEPPER FLAKES

1 CUP CANNED CRUSHED TOMATOES

10 PITTED OIL-CURED BLACK OLIVES, COARSELY CHOPPED

2 TABLESPOONS CAPERS, DRAINED

2 OUNCES HIGH-QUALITY OIL-PACKED TUNA, DRAINED AND FINELY FLAKED

SALT AND PEPPER

2 TABLESPOONS CHOPPED FRESH PARSLEY

1. Bring a large pot of salted water to a boil. Add the spaghetti and cook according to package directions.

2. Meanwhile, heat the olive oil in a skillet over medium heat. Add the onion, garlic, and red pepper flakes and cook until the garlic just begins to turn golden, 3 to 4 minutes. Add the tomatoes, olives, capers, and tuna and bring to a simmer. Reduce the heat, season with salt and pepper to taste, and continue cooking until the spaghetti is ready to serve.

3. Toss the drained spaghetti with the sauce and top with the parsley. Divide between 2 plates and serve immediately.

---

*I ain't a real cowboy, but I am one hell of a stud.* —JON VOIGHT, *MIDNIGHT COWBOY*, 1969

*Midnight Cowboy* was the first, and to date only, X-rated film ever to win a Best Picture Academy Award.

---

# GINGER-CITRUS SHRIMP WITH SUGAR SNAP PEAS

SERVES 2

*My dear friend, there's a little bit of Don Juan in every man,*
*and since I am Don Juan, there must be more of it in me!*

ERROL FLYNN, *ADVENTURES OF DON JUAN*, 1948

☆　☆　☆

Famous for his romantic exploits, and a real-life Don Juan, Giovanni Giacomo Casanova wrote a book on his adventures. Casanova enjoyed shellfish, champagne, and truffles before passionate encounters, popularizing the notion that they were aphrodisiacs. It was said of Casanova that at seventy-three, although he might not have been quite as strong in the bedroom, he was certainly still a "wolf at table."

He would have surely approved of this light and stimulating appetizer, with a tingling taste of citrus.

GRATED ZEST AND JUICE OF 1 LEMON

GRATED ZEST AND JUICE OF 2 NAVEL ORANGES

2 GARLIC CLOVES, MINCED

2 TABLESPOONS MINCED FRESH GINGER

½ TEASPOON SALT

8 LARGE SHRIMP, PEELED AND DEVEINED, TAILS LEFT ON

2 TABLESPOONS LEMON CURD

2 TEASPOONS CHOPPED FRESH CHIVES

1 TEASPOON CHOPPED FRESH CILANTRO

8 SUGAR SNAP PEAS, BLANCHED

1. In a saucepan, bring the lemon and orange zest and juices, garlic, 1 tablespoon of the ginger, and the salt to a rolling boil over high heat. Stir in the shrimp, cover, and remove from the heat. Let stand, covered, for 4 minutes. With a slotted spoon, transfer the shrimp to a plate, cover, and refrigerate until ready to serve.

2. Return the poaching liquid to a boil over medium-high heat. Cook until the liquid is reduced and very thick, about 12 minutes. Remove from the heat and add the remaining 1 tablespoon ginger and the lemon curd and stir until smooth. Stir in the chives and cilantro, transfer to a bowl, and refrigerate until ready to serve.

3. To serve, arrange the shrimp and sugar snap peas alternately around a plate, with the citrus sauce in the center for dipping.

*I don't even know him. I'm having all these fantasies about a man I never met.*
—MEG RYAN, *SLEEPLESS IN SEATTLE*, 1993

*Sleepless in Seattle* quotes another romantic movie, *An Affair to Remember,* which starred Deborah Kerr and Cary Grant and has the memorable line "Winter must be cold for those with no warm memories." In both *An Affair to Remember* and *Sleepless in Seattle,* the couples are supposed to meet at the top of the Empire State Building.

*You know where I was? Taking a bath in champagne.* —JOANNE WOODWARD, *A NEW KIND OF LOVE*, 1963

Joanne Woodward and Paul Newman follow Laurence Olivier and Vivien Leigh as the only married couple to win Oscars. Joanne Woodward won hers in 1958 for *The Three Faces of Eve;* Paul Newman didn't receive his until almost thirty years later, for *The Color of Money.* Woodward and Newman have appeared together in the films *The Long, Hot Summer* (1958), *Rally 'Round the Flag, Boys!* (1958), *A New Kind of Love* (1963), *The Drowning Pool* (1975), *Harry and Son* (1984), and *Mr. and Mrs. Bridge* (1990).

# ASPARAGUS ITALIAN-STYLE

SERVES 2

*—I love you.*

*—Snap out of it!*

NICOLAS CAGE AND CHER, *MOONSTRUCK*, 1987

☆   ☆   ☆

Since ancient Roman times, asparagus has been considered to be an aphrodisiac. Ovid, the famous Roman poet, thought that asparagus, as well as onions, honey, and pine nuts, stimulated the libido. Inspired by the ancient Romans, I've joined those ingredients in this easy-to-prepare delectable side dish.

| | |
|---|---|
| 8 OUNCES ASPARAGUS, ENDS REMOVED | SALT AND PEPPER |
| ½ SMALL ONION, THINLY SLICED | 2 TABLESPOONS DRIED BREAD CRUMBS |
| 1 TABLESPOON EXTRA-VIRGIN OLIVE OIL | 2 TABLESPOONS PINE NUTS |
| 1 TABLESPOON HONEY | 1 TABLESPOON GRATED PARMESAN CHEESE |

1. Preheat the oven to 375 degrees.

2. Place a sheet of aluminum foil on a work surface. Layer the asparagus and onion on the center of the foil, making a narrow stack. Drizzle the olive oil and honey over the vegetables and enclose in the foil, forming an airtight pouch. Bake for 5 minutes.

3. Remove the packet from the oven and preheat the broiler. Carefully open the packet and, using a fork, spread the asparagus and onion out into 1 layer. Season with salt and pepper and broil for about 4 minutes, or until the edges of the asparagus are crispy. Sprinkle with the bread crumbs and pine nuts and broil for about 2 minutes, or until golden.

4. Top with the Parmesan and serve.

---

*Of all the gin joints in all the towns in all the world, she walks into mine.* —HUMPHREY BOGART, *CASABLANCA*, 1942

*Casablanca* director Michael Curtiz had a thick Hungarian accent, which led to many amusing misunderstandings on the set. According to one legend, the prop man thought Mr. Curtiz had asked for a poodle, only to be scolded when it was clear that the director had wanted a puddle, not a poodle. Although Mr. Curtiz was nominated for Best Director for *Angels with Dirty Faces* and *Four Daughters,* he didn't win until *Casablanca.* Again, his limited English caused a few laughs when in his acceptance speech he said, "So many times I have a speech ready, but no dice. Always a bridesmaid, never a mother."

# BEEF TENDERLOIN WITH PINK PEPPERCORN SAUCE

*Why am I always at weddings and never actually getting married?*

HUGH GRANT, *FOUR WEDDINGS AND A FUNERAL*, 1994

☆　☆　☆

Always a bridesmaid, but never a bride: Richard Burton and Peter O'Toole, each with seven nominations, and Kirk Douglas, with three, have never won Oscars. Honorary Academy Awards don't count!

For a classic main course, beef tenderloin is always a winner. This tantalizing combination of tender beef with rich pink peppercorn sauce is sure to be nominated as one of your all-time favorite dishes.

1 TABLESPOON EXTRA-VIRGIN OLIVE OIL

TWO ¾-INCH-THICK BEEF TENDERLOINS (ABOUT 4 OUNCES EACH)

SALT AND PEPPER

¼ CUP RUBY PORT

1 TEASPOON PINK PEPPERCORNS

⅛ TEASPOON GROUND GINGER

2 TEASPOONS HEAVY CREAM

1 TABLESPOON BUTTER, DICED

1. In a small nonstick skillet, heat the olive oil over medium-high heat. Generously season both sides of the tenderloins with salt and pepper and place in the pan. Cook, turning once, until the edges are charred, about 2 minutes per side for medium. Transfer the tenderloins to a plate and cover.

2. Reduce the heat to medium-low and add the port, peppercorns, and ginger to the skillet, scraping up any bits left in the pan with a wooden spoon. Cook until the port is reduced by half, about 1 minute. Stir in the cream until simmering, then remove from the heat and add the butter, stirring until the butter is melted and the sauce is smooth. Season with additional salt and pepper to taste.

3. Put the tenderloins on 2 serving plates and stir any juices they have expelled into the sauce. Pour the sauce over the top and serve immediately.

---

*—Is it true that married people live longer?*

*—No, it just seems longer.*

—AN UNCREDITED ACTOR AND W. C. FIELDS, *THE BANK DICK*, 1940

There are many famous married Hollywood couples, including Elizabeth Taylor and Richard Burton, Joanne Woodward and Paul Newman, and Humphrey Bogart and Lauren Bacall. Katharine Hepburn and Spencer Tracy, as well as Jessica Lange and Sam Shepard, although together for many years, never married.

# JUST A BITE: ROMAINE LEAVES WITH RADISH VINAIGRETTE

SERVES 2

*Truly manly men do not dance.*

VOICE OF JOHN CUNNINGHAM AS INSTRUCTOR ON ALBUM, *IN AND OUT,* 1997

☆　☆　☆

Gay love has been portrayed in films such as *Four Weddings and a Funeral, The Birdcage, Love! Valour! Compassion!,* and *Far from Heaven. In and Out,* the story of a teacher who didn't realize he was gay, was inspired by the real-life story of Tom Hanks's high school drama teacher. With his teacher's permission, Hanks outed him during his 1994 acceptance speech for Best Actor for *Philadelphia.*

This slightly spicy palate-cleansing nibble is the perfect ending to any sort of romantic interlude.

1 TABLESPOON EXTRA-VIRGIN OLIVE OIL

2 TEASPOONS FRESHLY SQUEEZED LEMON JUICE

¼ TEASPOON SUGAR

2 RADISHES, FINELY MINCED

SALT AND PEPPER

4 INNER LEAVES OF ROMAINE LETTUCE

½ CUP ALFALFA SPROUTS

1. In a small bowl, whisk together the olive oil, lemon juice, sugar, and radishes until well combined. Season to taste with salt and pepper.

2. To assemble, divide the lettuce leaves between 2 plates. Top each leaf with a small pile of the sprouts and about 1 teaspoon of the dressing. Serve immediately.

---

*You should be kissed, and often, and by someone who knows how.* —CLARK GABLE, *GONE WITH THE WIND,* 1939

According to *The Guinness Book of Records,* the first leading lady to kiss another woman in a movie was Marlene Dietrich in *Morocco,* 1930. The first French kiss in a Hollywood film was between Natalie Wood and Warren Beatty in *Splendor in the Grass,* 1961. The longest film kiss was between Steve McQueen and Faye Dunaway in *The Thomas Crown Affair,* 1968, lasting for almost one minute.

---

# TIRAMISÙ

SERVES 2

*When women go wrong, men go right after them.*

MAE WEST, *SHE DONE HIM WRONG*, 1933

☆  ☆  ☆

Mae West began her film career in 1932 at age thirty-nine and starred with George Raft, Randolph Scott, W. C. Fields, and twice with Cary Grant. Despite being a censor's nightmare and playing loose women, she never once kissed on screen.

According to legend, tiramisù, which is Italian for "pick me up," was created by prostitutes as a snack between clients. In the movie *My Little Chickadee,* Mae West purred, "I generally avoid temptation, unless I can't resist it." Excellent dessert advice, especially when something as irresistible as this is on the menu.

6 LADYFINGERS
⅓ CUP COLD ESPRESSO
2 TABLESPOONS LIGHT OR DARK RUM
½ CUP MASCARPONE CHEESE
2 TABLESPOONS CONFECTIONERS' SUGAR
GRATED ZEST OF 1 LEMON
PINCH OF UNSWEETENED COCOA POWDER
PINCH OF GRATED NUTMEG

1. In a small bowl, break up the ladyfingers into very small pieces. Stir together the espresso and rum and sprinkle the mixture over the ladyfingers; toss the pieces lightly to absorb the liquid.

2. In another bowl, stir together the mascarpone, confectioners' sugar, and lemon zest until smooth.

3. Divide one-third of the ladyfingers between two 5-ounce ramekins or small cups. Top the ladyfingers with one-third of the mascarpone mixture, smoothing it evenly with a spoon. Repeat with 2 more layers of ladyfingers and mascarpone (you should end up with mascarpone on the top layer). Cover with plastic wrap and refrigerate for at least 2 hours.

4. Dust each ramekin with cocoa powder and nutmeg before serving.

Mae West is quoted as having said, "When I'm good, I'm very good, but when I'm bad, I'm better." Other sayings of hers include:

• It's not the men in your life that counts, it's the life in your men. (*I'm No Angel,* 1933)

• I wasn't always rich. No, there was a time I didn't know where my next husband was coming from. (*She Done Him Wrong,* 1933)

• Why don't you come up sometime and see me? (*She Done Him Wrong,* 1933)

• –Goodness, what beautiful diamonds!
–Goodness had nothing to do with it. (*Night After Night,* 1932)

# INDIVIDUAL KAHLÚA CHOCOLATE CAKES

SERVES 2

*It contains just a hint of chili pepper, to awaken the passions.*

JULIETTE BINOCHE, *CHOCOLAT,* 2000

☆  ☆  ☆

In *Chocolat,* Juliette Binoche plays the proprietor of a sinfully delicious chocolate shop who follows the ancient Mexican practice of mixing hot spices into chocolate. This seductive dessert, topped with a bit of cayenne pepper, is sure to warm your heart.

2 TABLESPOONS UNSALTED BUTTER

1 TABLESPOON UNSWEETENED COCOA POWDER, PLUS MORE DUSTING

2 OUNCES UNSWEETENED CHOCOLATE, FINELY CHOPPED

3 TABLESPOONS SUGAR

2 TABLESPOONS SLICED ALMONDS

¼ CUP KAHLÚA OR OTHER COFFEE LIQUEUR

1 LARGE EGG

1 TABLESPOON ALMOND BUTTER OR CREAMY PEANUT BUTTER

CAYENNE PEPPER

1. Preheat the oven to 350 degrees. Lightly butter two ½-cup ramekins and dust with cocoa powder. Put the ramekins in a deep baking dish and set aside.

2. In a large bowl set over a pan of gently simmering water, melt the butter and chocolate together and stir until smooth. Take the bowl off the heat and allow the mixture to cool to room temperature.

3. In a food processor, pulse the sugar, almonds, and cocoa powder together until very fine. Set aside.

4. When the chocolate mixture has cooled, whisk in the Kahlúa until smooth. Add the egg and almond butter and whisk until well blended. Sprinkle in the sugar mixture and briskly whisk until the sugar is dissolved. Divide the batter between the prepared ramekins. Pour hot water into the baking dish until it reaches halfway up the sides of the ramekins. Bake for 20 minutes, or until set.

5. Carefully remove the ramekins from the water bath and allow to cool for at least 10 minutes before inverting onto dessert plates.

6. Serve warm or at room temperature, each sprinkled with a pinch of cayenne.

*You played it for her, you can play it for me. Play it! Play it, Sam.* —HUMPHREY BOGART, *CASABLANCA, 1942.*

This is probably the most misquoted line in any movie, often remembered as "Play it again, Sam," which became the title of a film by Woody Allen. The actor who played Sam, Dooley Wilson, was really a professional drummer who copied the hand movements of the musician actually playing the piano behind the scenes.

The closing scene of *Casablanca* was filmed without a firm script and shot with several different endings so that not even the stars knew if Ilsa would stay or not.

# STRAWBERRIES WITH BALSAMIC VINEGAR

SERVES 2

*I appreciate this whole seduction scene you've got going on here,*
*but let me give you a tip: I'm a sure thing.*

JULIA ROBERTS, *PRETTY WOMAN*, 1990

☆ ☆ ☆

Strawberries, with their red color and heart shape, have long been associated with passion. You will certainly be passionate about the wonderful taste combination of strawberries and balsamic vinegar, popular in romantic Italy. Makes a perfect appetizer, too.

1 PINT LARGE STRAWBERRIES

1 TABLESPOON BALSAMIC VINEGAR

2 TABLESPOONS LIGHT BROWN SUGAR

1. Rinse the strawberries in cold water and drain, but leave on the stems and top leaves. Arrange on a serving plate.

2. Just prior to serving, sprinkle with the balsamic vinegar and top with the brown sugar.

---

*If I could find a real-life place to make me feel like Tiffany's, then I'd buy some furniture and give the cat a name.* —AUDREY HEPBURN, *BREAKFAST AT TIFFANY'S*, 1961

At the start of *Breakfast at Tiffany's,* Holly Golightly, one of the best character names ever, nibbles a Danish in front of the window of the famed store. A premier jewelry store in New York City since the 1800s, Tiffany's was the actual site of the movie's filming, including the interior scenes, which were shot when the store was closed.

Truman Capote, author of the novella the movie is based on, had envisioned Marilyn Monroe for the part of Holly Golightly. Although Audrey Hepburn was highly acclaimed by critics for her role, she herself questioned the wisdom of the casting choice.

Directed by Blake Edwards, with memorable music such as "Moon River" by Henry Mancini, this is one of Hollywood's finest romantic classics.

---

# CANDLELIT SUPPER

*You know how to whistle, don't you? You just put your lips together and . . . blow.*

—LAUREN BACALL, *TO HAVE AND HAVE NOT,* 1944

You might like to serve your romantic dinner for two on a small table in front of the fireplace, or if you don't have a fireplace, lay out a picnic blanket in the living room and set out lots of candles.

I leave the rest to your imagination.

## Movie Suggestions

*About Last Night . . . ,* 1986. Comedy about relationships, based on a David Mamet play. Stars Demi Moore, Rob Lowe, and James Belushi.

*Adam's Rib,* 1949. Must-see classic filled with witty dialogue, starring Katharine Hepburn and Spencer Tracy.

*The American President,* 1995. Michael Douglas plays a widower president of the United States in love with a lobbyist, Annette Bening.

*The Apartment,* 1960. Jack Lemmon lends his apartment to philandering executives and falls in love with his boss's girlfriend, Shirley MacLaine.

*Arthur,* 1981. Dudley Moore plays a drunken billionaire who falls for a simple waitress, Liza Minnelli. John Gielgud received an Oscar for his hilarious supporting role.

*Breakfast at Tiffany's,* 1961. Audrey Hepburn stars as an eccentric free spirit in this romantic comedy by Truman Capote.

*Bull Durham,* 1988. Romantic comedy starring Kevin Costner as a minor-league baseball player in love with Susan Sarandon.

*Casablanca,* 1942. Classic starring Humphrey Bogart and Ingrid Bergman.

*Cinderella Liberty,* 1973. James Caan plays a sailor in love with a prostitute, Marsha Mason.

*Desire,* 1936. Marlene Dietrich, a jewel thief, falls in love with good guy Gary Cooper. A classic.

*The English Patient,* 1996. Bittersweet story set during World War II.

*A Farewell to Arms,* 1932. Based on Ernest Hemingway's novel about the love between an English military nurse and an American ambulance driver.

*Four Weddings and a Funeral,* 1994. Confirmed bachelor Hugh Grant attends weddings but never as the groom.

*Frankie and Johnny,* 1991. Ex-con Al Pacino falls in love with a jaded waitress, Michelle Pfeiffer.

*Ghost,* 1990. Patrick Swayze, Demi Moore, and Whoopi Goldberg star in a story of love beyond death.

*Groundhog Day,* 1993. Bill Murray keeps reliving the same day until he earns the love and respect of his heart's desire, Andie MacDowell.

*High Fidelity,* 2000. Romantic comedy, with a brilliant supporting-actor performance by Jack Black, about a record-store owner's quest for love. Stars John Cusack.

*Indiscreet,* 1958. Love story starring Cary Grant and Ingrid Bergman.

*It Happened One Night,* 1934. Classic romantic comedy starring Claudette Colbert and Clark Gable.

*It Started with Eve,* 1941. Charming love story.

*The Long, Hot Summer,* 1958. The first film Paul Newman and Joanne Woodward made together, based on a William Faulkner novel.

*Love Affair,* 1939. Tearjerker about lovers who promise to meet on top of the Empire State Building once their other affairs are settled. Stars Irene Dunne and Charles Boyer. Remade in 1957 as *An Affair to Remember,* starring Cary Grant and Deborah Kerr. Both are must-see classics.

*Love Among the Ruins,* 1975. Millionaire widower Laurence Olivier is hired to defend Katharine Hepburn, whom he has secretly loved for decades, in a lawsuit.

*Moonstruck,* 1987. Charming romantic comedy starring Cher and Nicolas Cage.

*The Owl and the Pussycat,* 1970. Barbra Streisand, in her first nonsinging role, plays a hooker who falls for an intellectual.

*Pillow Talk,* 1959. Classic fifties comedy starring Doris Day and Rock Hudson.

*Pretty Woman,* 1990. Cinderella story with Julia Roberts as a sweet-hearted hooker who falls for Prince Charming, Richard Gere.

*Roman Holiday,* 1953. Audrey Hepburn stars as a young princess escaping her royal duties for one day.

*A Room with a View,* 1986. Academy Award–winning must-see romantic tale based on E. M. Forster's novel.

*Same Time, Next Year,* 1978. Twenty-six-year love affair between Ellen Burstyn and Alan Alda, who meet only one weekend each year.

*The Seven Year Itch,* 1955. Classic Marilyn Monroe sex comedy.

*Sleepless in Seattle,* 1993. Charming romantic comedy starring Meg Ryan and Tom Hanks.

*There's Something About Mary,* 1998. Offbeat zany comedy starring Cameron Diaz and Ben Stiller. Many memorable moments.

*Tin Cup,* 1996. Kevin Costner stars as a golfer whose game and life are helped by psychologist Rene Russo.

*The Truth About Cats and Dogs,* 1996. Intelligent romantic comedy, sort of a female *Cyrano de Bergerac,* with Uma Thurman trading places with Janeane Garofalo.

*The Way We Were,* 1973. Story of a twenty-year star-crossed romance, starring Barbra Streisand and Robert Redford.

*When Harry Met Sally,* 1989. Billy Crystal and Meg Ryan star in this romantic comedy with the famous line "I'll have what she's having."

# FAMILY MOVIE NIGHT

### COMING ATTRACTIONS
COWS IN THE GRASS ★ RAW VEGGIES WITH FLUFFY DIP ★ DOG CHIPS ★ BUG JUICE

### FEATURE PRESENTATION
CRUNCHY CHICKEN NUGGETS ★ POPCORN SHRIMP
OVEN-ROASTED VEGGIES ★ POTATO WEDGES WITH CHILI-MAPLE KETCHUP

### THE CONCESSION STAND
FROZEN PEANUT BUTTER AND JELLY SANDWICHES ★ FRUIT KEBABS WITH CREAMY MARSHMALLOW SAUCE
MARSHMALLOWS WITH CHOCOLATY PEANUT BUTTER DIP

### LIGHTS, CAMERA, ACTION! DINNER IN A POPCORN BOWL
MOVIE SUGGESTIONS

*Insanity runs in my family. . . . It practically gallops.*

—CARY GRANT, *ARSENIC AND OLD LACE*, 1944

The inspiration for this chapter came from my husband, Marc. It all started about five years ago, when he wanted to give me time off from the kids and a night off from cooking.

During my free afternoon, while I was hiking with a friend, Marc and the kids rented movies and went grocery shopping. They brought the TV out onto our front porch and set up all the dinner provisions by the grill.

I was skeptical at first, thinking he'd take the easy way out with frozen dinners or takeout. This was, after all, the man who seriously asks where we keep the ice and whose motto is the line from *The Odd Couple* "You don't have to cook. I have enough potato chips to last a year."

To my utter shock, the meal was great. Succulent swordfish with guacamole, perfectly grilled corn on the cob, salad with my daughter's buttermilk and chive dressing concoction, and, for dessert, ice cream with a choice of three toppings. We ate on paper plates, so cleanup was a snap. The two movies they picked were terrific—*Ghostbusters* and *The Princess Bride*—and we all had a great time.

My husband and the kids were so proud of their newfound cooking skills that they did it all again the next week. From then on, it became a weekly event. A family ritual, Movie Festival Night, was born at the Segans'.

The following kid-friendly foods can be eaten family-style, with each course served in a different popcorn bowl, passed around, and shared. No plates, no forks, less cleanup, and more fun.

Of course, just because you're serving the entire meal in popcorn bowls doesn't mean you can't serve popcorn, too. For variety, I like to set out powdered popcorn toppings with ingredients from my spice shelf, such as cinnamon sugar, powdered Cheddar cheese, and Cajun dry rub, so everyone can custom-design their popcorn.

# COWS IN THE GRASS

SERVES 8

*—You want . . . brown sandwiches . . . or green sandwiches?*

*—What's the green?*

*—It's either very new cheese or very old meat.*

WALTER MATTHAU AND HERB EDELMAN, *THE ODD COUPLE*, 1968

☆　☆　☆

We've all had Pigs in a Blanket; well, my version is Cows in the Grass, string cheese topped with either sprouts, spinach, or chives and wrapped in refrigerator crescent rolls. A warm, melty, satisfying movie snack. You can sprinkle on powdered spices such as Cajun dry rub or garlic powder before rolling your cow in the grass if you like.

ONE 8-OUNCE PACKAGE REFRIGERATOR CRESCENT ROLLS

¼ CUP FROZEN CHOPPED SPINACH, THAWED AND DRAINED

FRESH ALFALFA SPROUTS

2 TABLESPOONS CHOPPED FRESH CHIVES

FOUR 1-OUNCE STICKS OF STRING CHEESE

1. Preheat the oven to 375 degrees.

2. Unroll the crescent-roll dough and separate into 8 triangles. Spread a combination of the spinach, sprouts, and chives over each dough triangle, or use each "grass" filling separately. Cut the sticks of string cheese in half, place a cheese section at the wide end of each dough triangle, and roll. Transfer to an ungreased baking sheet and bake for about 12 minutes, or until golden. Allow to cool slightly before serving.

---

*Imagine being remembered around the world for the invention of a mouse!* —WALT DISNEY

Mickey Mouse first appeared in 1928 in the black-and-white cartoon short *Steamboat Willie,* inspired by the 1928 Buster Keaton movie *Steamboat Bill, Jr.*

---

# RAW VEGGIES WITH FLUFFY DIP

SERVES 6

*Ehh, what's up, Doc?*

BUGS BUNNY

☆   ☆   ☆

Mel Blanc, who provided the voices for Warner Bros. characters such as Bugs Bunny, Daffy Duck, Porky Pig, Speedy Gonzales, and Tweety and Sylvester, ad-libbed the now-famous Bugs Bunny line, originally written as "Hey, what's cooking?" Bugs Bunny, that "wascally wabbit," featured in hundreds of cartoons, won an Oscar in 1959 for *Knighty Knight Bugs* and made a guest appearance in the hilarious 1988 movie *Who Framed Roger Rabbit*.

This dip, great with carrots and other raw veggies, is sensational made with fresh whipped cream, but it's good with the ready-whipped type, too, if you're in a rush.

¾ CUP HEAVY CREAM

½ TEASPOON DRY MUSTARD

½ TEASPOON SALT

2 TABLESPOONS SOUR CREAM

2 TEASPOONS WHOLE GRAIN MUSTARD

CELERY AND CARROT STICKS OR OTHER RAW VEGETABLES

1. In a large bowl, using an electric mixer, whip the cream with the dry mustard and salt until it forms soft peaks. Then stir in the sour cream and whole grain mustard until combined.

2. Serve with celery and carrot sticks.

---

*Great, Chewie, great. Always thinking with your stomach.*

—HARRISON FORD, *STAR WARS: RETURN OF THE JEDI*, 1983

There have been five *Star Wars* films to date, beginning with *Star Wars* in 1977 and followed by *The Empire Strikes Back* (1980), *Return of the Jedi* (1983), *The Phantom Menace* (1999), and *Attack of the Clones* (2002).

*Star Wars* trivia:

• Kurt Russell, Nick Nolte, and Christopher Walken were all briefly considered for the role of Han Solo, ultimately played by Harrison Ford.

• Chewbacca's voice was created from a composite of several animals, including a walrus, a bear, and a camel.

• Sissy Spacek was originally cast as Princess Leia, and Carrie Fisher was to star in the movie *Carrie*. However, since Fisher didn't want to do the nude scene in *Carrie* and Spacek didn't mind, they switched roles.

• Harrison Ford's reply to Leia's declaration of love in *The Empire Strikes Back* was ad-libbed. After several unsuccessful takes, Ford substituted the line "I know" for the scripted "I love you, too."

# DOG CHIPS

SERVES 6

*Strange as it may seem, they give ballplayers nowadays very peculiar names. . . .*

*Now, on the St. Louis team we have Who's on first,*

*What's on second, I Don't Know is on third.*

BUD ABBOTT, *THE NAUGHTY NINETIES*, 1945

☆  ☆  ☆

Hot dogs and baseball, perfect together. Enjoy these easy-to-make potato-chip-crusted hot dogs while watching your favorite baseball movies, like *Angels in the Outfield, The Bad News Bears, Field of Dreams, A League of Their Own,* and *The Rookie.*

4 HOT DOGS, CUT INTO ½-INCH-THICK SLICES

2 TABLESPOONS KETCHUP, MUSTARD, OR MAYONNAISE, OR A COMBINATION

ONE 1½-OUNCE BAG POTATO CHIPS, CRUSHED

1. Preheat the oven to 350 degrees.

2. In a bowl, toss the hot dog slices with the condiment of your choice until completely coated. Pour the potato chip crumbs onto a plate and roll the condiment-coated hot dog slices in the crumbs until well coated. Put the crumb-coated hot dog slices on an ungreased baking sheet and bake for 10 minutes, or until golden.

3. Serve with toothpicks and extra condiments for dipping.

---

*I'll have three burgers, three apple pies, and three shakes. What do you guys want?*

—DREW BARRYMORE, *CHARLIE'S ANGELS*, 2000

The first fast-food hamburger restaurant in America wasn't McDonald's or Burger King. It was White Castle, which opened in the 1920s.

# BUG JUICE

SERVES 4

*Waiter, I'm in my soup!*

VOICE OF JOHN RATZENBERGER, *A BUG'S LIFE*, 1998

☆　☆　☆

Plain seltzer and your favorite flavor of jelly can make an instant homemade soda. Serve it with these yummy gummy-worm ice cubes, which the little ones can pretend are fossils.

1¼ CUPS LEMONADE

6 GUMMY WORMS

ONE 8-OUNCE JAR GRAPE JELLY

2 CUPS SELTZER

1. Pour 1 cup of the lemonade into a plastic ice-cube tray. Cut the gummy worms in half and put 1 in each cube section, with the cut end submerged and the tail end hanging out. Freeze until firm.

2. When ready to serve, put the remaining ¼ cup lemonade and the grape jelly into a blender and blend until smooth. Divide the grape syrup among 4 glasses and fill with the seltzer. Put 3 worm cubes into each glass and serve.

# CRUNCHY CHICKEN NUGGETS

SERVES 6

*You will join me for dinner! That's not a request!*

VOICE OF ROBBY BENSON, *BEAUTY AND THE BEAST*, 1991

☆ ☆ ☆

*Beauty and the Beast* is the only animated film to be nominated for a Best Picture Academy Award. With these delicious cereal-and-cracker-coated chicken nuggets on the menu, you'll never have to be a beast about getting your kids to the table again.

VEGETABLE OIL

ALL-PURPOSE FLOUR

SALT AND PEPPER

1½ CUPS CRISPY RICE CEREAL

½ CUP CHEDDAR-CHEESE-FLAVORED CRACKERS

1 POUND BONELESS, SKINLESS CHICKEN BREASTS

1 LARGE EGG, BEATEN WITH 2 TEASPOONS OF WATER

1. Preheat the oven to 400 degrees. Lightly oil a large baking sheet and set aside.

2. Put flour on a shallow plate and season generously with salt and pepper. On a large plate, crush the cereal and crackers together into coarse crumbs.

3. Cut the chicken into 1-inch cubes. Working a few pieces at a time, dredge the chicken cubes first in the flour, then in the egg, and finally in the cereal-cracker mixture. Place the coated cubes ½ inch apart on the baking sheet.

4. Bake for about 12 minutes, or until the chicken is cooked through and the coating is golden. Serve in a large popcorn bowl.

---

*One morning I shot an elephant in my pajamas. How he got in my pajamas, I don't know.*

—GROUCHO MARX, *ANIMAL CRACKERS*, 1930

The Marx Brothers, despite having made such memorable movies as *Animal Crackers, Duck Soup, Horse Feathers, A Night at the Opera, A Day at the Races,* and *Monkey Business,* never won an Oscar. Groucho Marx was, however, recognized by the Academy with an Honorary Award in 1973.

A sampling of lines from their classic comedies include:

- Look at me. . . . I worked my way up from nothing to a state of extreme poverty. (*Monkey Business,* 1931)

- You've got the brain of a four-year-old boy, and I bet he was glad to get rid of it. (*Horse Feathers,* 1932)

- Don't wake him up. He's got insomnia—he's trying to sleep it off. (*A Night at the Opera,* 1935)

- Marry me, and I'll never look at any other horse. (*A Day at the Races,* 1937)

# POPCORN SHRIMP

SERVES 6

*All my life I've been waiting for someone,*
*and when I find her . . . she's a fish!*

TOM HANKS, *SPLASH*, 1984

☆   ☆   ☆

We've all enjoyed popcorn shrimp, those tiny batter-coated, fried morsels. My version is made with shrimp and actual popcorn, baked, not fried, until crisp and golden.

I was inspired to create this recipe after an interesting event. Actor Christopher Walken shot a short film in our apartment, which he had written and was directing for Showtime. Entitled *Popcorn Shrimp,* it involved Walken's own special recipe and a funny plot of mistaken identity. At some point toward the end of the shoot, Walken, who had overheard that my son, Max, loves shrimp, offered him one. Max tried the shrimp and immediately made a face. Surprised by my son's negative reaction, Walken took a taste, realized it wasn't good, and turned accusingly to the actor who had prepared the shrimp. The actor sheepishly explained, "Well, I was only acting. I can't cook, I can only *act* like I'm cooking."

4 CUPS UNSALTED POPCORN

3 TABLESPOONS MILK

1 LARGE EGG

2 TABLESPOONS ALL-PURPOSE FLOUR

2 TABLESPOONS CORNFLAKE CRUMBS

½ TEASPOON SALT

1 TEASPOON BAKING POWDER

1 POUND COOKED MEDIUM SHRIMP WITH TAILS LEFT ON

1. Preheat the oven to 450 degrees. Lightly grease a large nonstick baking sheet and set aside.

2. Put the popcorn into a sturdy plastic bag and crush it with a rolling pin or a heavy skillet. Transfer to a bowl.

3. In another bowl, whisk together the milk, egg, flour, cornflake crumbs, salt, and baking powder until well combined.

4. Dip each shrimp, holding it by the tail, into the batter, shaking off any excess. Roll in the crushed popcorn and place on the baking sheet. Repeat until all the shrimp are coated, spacing them evenly in 1 layer on the sheet.

5. Bake for about 10 minutes, or until the coating is golden brown. Serve warm in a large popcorn bowl.

*Magic Mirror, on the wall, who is the fairest of them all?*

—VOICE OF LUCILLE LA VERNE, *SNOW WHITE AND THE SEVEN DWARFS*, 1937

Made by Walt Disney in 1937, *Snow White and the Seven Dwarfs* was Hollywood's first feature-length animated movie. It earned Walt Disney an Oscar, or rather, several. The Academy presented Disney with a normal-sized Oscar and seven tiny ones in recognition of this outstanding film.

Awful, Dirty, Gloomy, Jumpy, and Shifty were possible names considered for the dwarfs.

# OVEN-ROASTED VEGGIES

SERVES 6

*—Ogres are like onions.*

*—They stink?*

*—Yes. No!*

*—Oh, they make you cry.*

*—No! . . . Layers! Onions have layers. Ogres have layers.*

*Onions have layers. You get it? We both have layers.*

*—Oh, you both have layers. Oh. You know, not everybody likes onions.*

VOICES OF MIKE MYERS AND EDDIE MURPHY, *SHREK*, 2001

☆   ☆   ☆

Veggies become incredibly delicious when baked, tasting almost like chips. If you like, add a sliced red onion to the mix. Onion loses its sharpness and becomes candy-sweet with roasting.

OLIVE OIL

8 OUNCES STRING BEANS

4 CUPS SMALL CAULIFLOWER FLORETS

4 CUPS SMALL BROCCOLI FLORETS

4 LARGE CARROTS, CUT DIAGONALLY INTO ½-INCH SLICES

SALT AND PEPPER

1. Preheat the oven to 425 degrees. Lightly oil 2 large nonstick baking sheets and arrange the vegetables in a single layer on the pans.

2. Bake for about 30 minutes, or until the vegetables are crisp at the edges and cooked through.

3. Season to taste with salt and pepper. Serve in large popcorn bowls.

> *All right, nobody move. I've got a dragon and I'm not afraid to use it.* —VOICE OF EDDIE MURPHY, *SHREK*, 2001
>
> *Shrek* was the first movie to win an Oscar for Best Animated Feature, a new category added to the Academy Awards in 2002. Interestingly, the main voice actors, Mike Myers, Eddie Murphy, and Cameron Diaz, never actually worked together. Their parts were recorded separately with readers feeding the actors the other characters' lines.

# POTATO WEDGES WITH CHILI-MAPLE KETCHUP

SERVES 6

*Please let it be a Mrs. Potato Head. . . . Hey, I can dream, can't I?*

VOICE OF DON RICKLES, *TOY STORY*, 1995

☆　☆　☆

*Toy Story,* the first completely computer-generated feature-length movie, stars classic toys, including Slinky, Etch A Sketch, and Mr. Potato Head, which originally used real potatoes. I toyed around a little myself and created this delicious slightly spicy-sweet dip for oven-baked potato wedges.

EXTRA-VIRGIN OLIVE OIL

4 LARGE POTATOES, UNPEELED, HALVED LENGTHWISE AND CUT INTO 8 WEDGES

SALT AND PEPPER

¼ CUP KETCHUP

2 TABLESPOONS PURE MAPLE SYRUP

½ TEASPOON CHILI POWDER

1. Preheat the oven to 500 degrees. Generously oil a baking sheet and place on the center rack for 10 minutes. Toss the potato wedges with a tablespoon or two of olive oil.

2. Arrange the wedges in a single layer on the hot sheet. Bake, turning once, for 25 to 30 minutes, until the potatoes are cooked through and golden. Season to taste with salt and pepper.

3. While the potatoes are cooking, prepare the dip. In a small serving bowl, mix together the ketchup, maple syrup, and chili powder until well combined.

4. Serve the potato wedges in a large popcorn bowl with the dip on the side.

---

*The world is changed. I feel it in the water. I feel it in the earth. I smell it in the air. Much that once was is lost, for none now live who remember it.* —KATE BLANCHETT, *THE LORD OF THE RINGS: THE FELLOWSHIP OF THE RING*, 2001

A short-lived fad was Smell-O-Vision or Aromarama, films that released fragrances to match the plot. The 1960 film *Scent of Mystery* treated the audience to scents such as tobacco, garlic, wine, peaches, and the ocean. The film's tag line explained that films first moved in 1895, that they then talked in 1927, and that "now they smell!"

# FROZEN PEANUT BUTTER AND JELLY SANDWICHES

MAKES ABOUT 2 DOZEN MINI FROZEN TREATS

*It's sandwich day! Every Thursday I take Pudge the fish a peanut butter sandwich.*

VOICE OF DAVEIGH CHASE, *LILO AND STITCH*, 2002

☆   ☆   ☆

Elvis Presley fans will certainly enjoy *Lilo and Stitch,* the animated movie that features many of Presley's hits, such as "Heartbreak Hotel," "Stuck on You," "Devil in Disguise," "Blue Hawaii," and "Hound Dog." The King, incidentally, loved peanut butter sandwiches fried in butter.

This simple-to-make frozen peanut butter and jelly filling is great sandwiched between your favorite cookies, such as graham crackers or shortbread.

½ CUP HEAVY CREAM

2 TABLESPOONS SUGAR

⅓ CUP CREAMY PEANUT BUTTER

2 TABLESPOONS GRAPE JELLY

ABOUT 48 GRAHAM CRACKERS, SHORTBREAD, OR VANILLA WAFERS

1. Whip the cream and sugar in a bowl, using an electric mixer, until the cream forms soft peaks. Add the peanut butter and continue blending until well combined. Add the grape jelly and blend for just a few seconds, until just swirled into the mixture.

2. Spoon the peanut butter and jelly cream between 2 of the cookies and place in a freezer-safe container. Repeat with the remaining cookies. Cover the container with plastic wrap and freeze until firm.

---

*C'mon, show a little backbone, will ya?* —FRED SORENSON, *RAIDERS OF THE LOST ARK*, 1981

The scene in *Raiders of the Lost Ark* when Indiana Jones pulls out a gun and shoots the guy who has just completed a series of threatening sword moves was originally supposed to be a very long fight scene between the two. However, Harrison Ford became ill during filming, and so he and director Steven Spielberg decided to cut the scene short by having Indy just shoot the sword guy.

# FRUIT KEBABS WITH CREAMY MARSHMALLOW SAUCE

SERVES 6

*I'm here to fight for truth, justice, and the American way.*

CHRISTOPHER REEVE, *SUPERMAN*, 1978

☆  ☆  ☆

Actors such as Christopher Reeve in *Superman* and Tobey Maguire in *Spiderman* got into condition for their superhero roles by following rigorous diet and exercise regimes.

These kid-pleasing treats make a super-healthy movie snack.

4 OUNCES CREAM CHEESE

¼ CUP HEAVY CREAM

½ CUP MARSHMALLOW CRÈME

1 TEASPOON VANILLA EXTRACT

2 TABLESPOONS CONFECTIONERS' SUGAR

ASSORTED BITE-SIZED FRUIT, SUCH AS BANANAS, PINEAPPLE, AND MELON, CUT INTO CHUNKS, AND GRAPES

6 LONG SKEWERS OR TOOTHPICKS

1. In a mixing bowl, using an electric mixer set on high, whip the cream cheese and heavy cream until fluffy and smooth. Add the marshmallow crème and continue beating until well combined. Add the vanilla extract and confectioners' sugar and beat until very smooth.

2. Transfer to a small bowl and serve with the fruit and skewers for dipping.

*I never drink when I fly.* —CHRISTOPHER REEVE, *SUPERMAN*, 1978

Besides the glasses, you can tell Superman and Clark Kent apart because they part their hair on different sides.

# MARSHMALLOWS WITH CHOCOLATY PEANUT BUTTER DIP

SERVES 6

*Yeah, give me a slice of anchovies and peanut butter.*

TEENAGE MUTANT NINJA TURTLES II, 1991

☆  ☆  ☆

Superheroes, comic book characters with extraordinary strength and abilities, have been represented in film in such early classics as *Adventures of Captain Marvel* (1941), *The Batman* (1943), *Captain America* (1944), and *Superman* (1948). This not-too-sweet dip is also super with fresh fruit.

¼ CUP CREAMY PEANUT BUTTER

3 TABLESPOONS MILK

2 TABLESPOONS CONFECTIONERS' SUGAR

3 TO 4 OUNCES SWEET MILK CHOCOLATE

18 LARGE MARSHMALLOWS

1. In a small bowl, using an electric mixer or a whisk, beat the peanut butter, milk, and confectioners' sugar until well combined. Transfer to a small serving bowl.

2. Using a grater, shave the chocolate onto a small plate.

3. Everyone can dip a marshmallow into the peanut butter mixture and then into the chocolate flakes, or you can predip and arrange the marshmallows on a serving platter.

---

*The ruby slippers, what have you done with them? Give them to me or I'll . . .*

—MARGARET HAMILTON, *THE WIZARD OF OZ*, 1939

Dorothy's ruby slippers were originally supposed to be silver, as in the book. However, it was decided that red looked better on film, so they were changed.

While the slipper-color change was purposeful, *The Wizard of Oz* has its share of bloopers. For example, during Dorothy's trip down the yellow brick road, you can see her hair change length at least three times. It gets noticeably longer when the witch is trying to take off Dorothy's slippers but becomes short again when everyone is at the witch's castle.

Another blooper is the line in which the Wicked Witch of the West mentions "the little insects" that were sent to slow down Dorothy and her trio of friends. Since the jitterbug scene with the insects was cut, so should have been the line.

# DINNER IN A POPCORN BOWL

*This is my family. . . .*

*It's little, and broken, but still good. Yeah, still good.*

—VOICE OF CHRIS SANDERS, *LILO AND STITCH,* 2002

**Y**ou can make your own rules on who counts as family for your family movie night. You can also make your own rules on who cooks, who rents the videos, who is invited, and who cleans up.

For our Movie Festival Night, Mom does *not* cook or clean up, the kids and Dad do. The kids get to pick the videos and usually rent three: one sure bet that they know the adults will like, one that they like, and a wild card, picked because of an interesting video box.

Besides the recipes in this chapter, you can offer an assortment of other snacks, like bowls of nuts or cheese cubes. If you have one of those never-opened chemistry kits around, maybe you can finally put the test tubes to good use. Fill them with flavored syrups and serve them with seltzer or ginger ale for make-your-own drinks. Set out some pop candy to add to the drinks for a bubbly surprise.

# Movie Suggestions

*The Absent-Minded Professor,* 1961, G. A professor, played by Fred MacMurray, accidentally invents a high-flying substance, "Flubber."

*Airplane!,* 1980, PG. Airplane-disaster spoof starring Leslie Nielsen.

*Austin Powers: International Man of Mystery,* 1997, PG-13. Warmhearted spoof on James Bond spy films.

*Babe,* 1995, G. A pig saves himself from slaughter by learning to herd sheep. Charming.

*Back to the Future,* 1985, PG. A time machine sends a teenager, played by Michael J. Fox, back in time to his parents' high school days.

*Batman,* 1989, PG-13. Stars Michael Keaton as Batman.

*Beauty and the Beast,* 1991, G. The first animated feature film to be nominated for an Academy Award as Best Picture.

*Bowfinger,* 1999, PG-13. Comedy starring Steve Martin and Eddie Murphy, about a filmmaker trying to make a movie including a big celeb without his knowing about it.

*Big,* 1988, PG. A kid gets his wish to be grown up. Stars Tom Hanks.

*Charlie's Angels,* 2000, PG-13. Stars Drew Barrymore, Cameron Diaz, and Lucy Liu. Based on the seventies TV hit.

*Chocolat,* 2000, PG-13. A woman and her daughter start a chocolate shop in a provincial French town. Delightful story, starring Johnny Depp.

*Edward Scissorhands,* 1990, PG-13. A scientist temporarily attaches scissors as hands on his young creation, only to die before replacing them. Sweet, visually interesting story.

*E.T. the Extra-Terrestrial,* 1982, PG. Classic about an alien trying to get back home.

*Galaxy Quest,* 1999, PG. Charming spoof of *Star Trek.*

*George of the Jungle,* 1997, PG. Stars Brendan Fraser as the lovable cartoon character of the sixties.

*Ghostbusters,* 1984, PG. Paranormal bounty-hunting. Great fun; a must-see family movie.

*Good Burger,* 1997, PG. Fast food and fun, featuring Nickelodeon stars Kenan Thompson and Kel Mitchell.

*Gremlins,* 1984, PG. Mogwai creatures, cute until wet, run amok in this comedy/horror movie by Steven Spielberg. A classic.

*Home Alone,* 1990, PG. Every kid's dream and parent's nightmare. Cute.

*Honey, I Shrunk the Kids,* 1989, G. Inventor-dad creates a shrinking machine, and his kids are accidentally reduced to itsy-bitsy size.

*Ice Age,* 2002, PG. Prehistoric animals coping with the coming Ice Age, with the voice of the sloth done by the hysterically funny comic John Leguizamo.

*James and the Giant Peach,* 1996, G. Great for little movie fans.

*Jurassic Park,* 1993, PG. Dinosaurs are created through technological advances to fill a theme park. An action thriller.

*The Karate Kid,* 1984, PG. A teenager, played by Ralph Macchio, is befriended by a karate expert, who teaches him more than the martial arts. A lovely classic.

*King Kong,* 1933, PG. A classic. Invite the grandparents over to watch it with you.

*Lilo and Stitch,* 2002, PG. Witty animated film about an alien adopted by two orphans.

*Matilda,* 1996, PG. Fantastic movie about a smart little girl stuck in a horrific school. Based on the book by Roald Dahl.

*Men in Black,* 1997, PG-13. Witty spoof on all those alien movies.

*Monsters, Inc.,* 2001, PG. Pixar animated movie. Great for those under twelve.

*Mighty Joe Young,* 1949; remade in 1998, PG. Both are great variations on the King Kong theme.

*Mrs. Doubtfire,* 1993, PG-13. Robin Williams is hysterical as a female-impersonating nanny to his own children.

*Oh, God!,* 1977, PG. John Denver is asked by God, played by George Burns, to help save the world.

*The Princess Bride,* 1987, PG. A fairy tale–like action adventure. Stars Mandy Patinkin, Wallace Shawn, Billy Crystal, Robin Wright, Peter Falk, and André the Giant.

*Raiders of the Lost Ark,* 1981, PG. An action-adventure classic. See it again!

*Rush Hour,* 1998, PG-13. Fun Jackie Chan action comedy.

*Shrek,* 2001, PG. Great voice-acting by Cameron Diaz, Mike Myers, and Eddie Murphy. Everyone in the family will enjoy this funny spoof on Disney animated movies, created by DreamWorks.

*Spider-Man,* 2002, PG-13. Marvel Comic hero brilliantly played by Tobey Maguire. Great fun.

*Star Wars,* 1977, PG. Sci-fi action classic.

*Superman,* 1978, PG. Stars Christopher Reeve as the man of steel, with Margot Kidder as Lois Lane.

*Teenage Mutant Ninja Turtles,* 1990, PG. Renaissance-artist-named turtles who are morphed into
  superheros. A fun movie.

*The Thief of Bagdad,* 1940. Must-see classic.

*Toy Story,* 1995, G. The toys' voices are wonderfully acted by Tom Hanks, Don Rickles, and Tim
  Allen. A funny, must-see look at the secret life of toys.

*Who Framed Roger Rabbit,* 1988, PG. A combination of animated and live action about a plot to rid
  the world of cartoons. Voices of Mel Blanc, Kathleen Turner, and others.

*Zoolander,* 2001, PG-13. Ben Stiller and Owen Wilson star in a comedy about male models.

# BIBLIOGRAPHY

Apicius. *Cookery and Dining in Imperial Rome.* Edited and translated by Joseph Doomers Vehling. New York: Dover Publications, 1977.

Apicius. *The Roman Cookery Book.* Translated by Barbara Flower and Elizabeth Rosenblaum. London: George G. Harrap and Co., 1958.

*Athenaeus. The Deipnosophists.* Bks. I–XV, *The Philosopher's Banquet.* Translated by C. B. Gulick. Loeb Classical Library. Cambridge: Harvard University Press, 1929.

Beecher, Catherine E. *Miss Beecher's Domestic Receipt Book.* New York: Harper and Brothers, 1858.

Beeton, Isabella. *The Book of Household Management.* London, S. D. Beeton, 1861.

*Booke of Cookerie. Otherwise called: The good Huswifes Handmaide for the Kitchin.* London: Edward Allde, 1597.

*Buckeye Cookery.* Minneapolis, 1885. Reprint of 1883 edition, New York: Dover, 1975.

Cato. "On Agriculture." In Cato and Varro, *On Agriculture,* translated by William Davis Hooper and revised by Harrison Boyd Ash. Loeb Classical Library. Cambridge: Harvard University Press, 1935.

Cicero, *On the Good Life.* Translated by M. Grant. Penguin Classics. New York: Penguin Books, 1971.

Cogan (also Coghan), Thomas. *The Haven of Health: Chiefly Gathered for the Comfort of Students, and Consequently of All those that have a Care of their Health.* London: 1584.

Cooper, Joseph (chief cook to Charles I). *The Art of Cookery Refin'd and Augmented.* London: 1654.

Corey, Melinda, and Ochoa, George. *The Dictionary of Film Quotations.* New York: Crown Trade Paperbacks, 1995.

Cornelius, Mrs. M. H. *The Young Housekeepers Friend.* Boston: Brown and Taggard, 1859.

Coryate, Thomas. *Coryates Crudities; hastily gobbled up in five months travels.* London: W. Stansby, 1611.

*Creole Cookery Book.* Edited by the Christian Women's Exchange of New Orleans. New Orleans: T. H. Thomason, 1885.

*Cuoco Napoletano. (The Neapolitan Recipe Collection).* Edited and Translated by Terence Scully. Ann Arbor: The University of Michigan Press, 2000.

Dawson, Thomas. *The Good Huswifes Jewell.* London: 1586.

Debo, Angie, ed. *The Cowman's Southwest: Being the Reminiscences of Oliver Nelson.* Lincoln: University of Nebraska Press, 1953.

De Worde, Wynkyn. *Boke of Keruynge.* London: 1513.

Escoffier, G. A. *A Guide to Modern Cookery.* New York: McClure, Phillips, 1907.

Estes, Rufus. *Good Things to Eat.* Chicago: Self-published, 1911.

Farmer, Fannie Merritt. *The Boston Cooking School Cook Book.* Boston: Little, Brown, 1896.

Fisher, Abby. *What Mrs. Fisher Knows About Old Southern Cooking.* 1881. Facsimile, Bedford, Mass.: Applewood Books, 1995.

Fisher, M. F. K. *How to Cook a Wolf.* (New York: World Publishing, 1942; New York: Northpoint Press, 1988.

*Forme of Cury, The: A Roll of Ancient Cookery, compiled about A.D. 1390.* Edited by Samuel Pegge. London: 1780.

Francatelli, Charles E. *The Modern Cook.* Philadelphia: T. B. Peterson and Brothers, 1853.

*Galen on Food and Diet.* Translated by M. Grant. New York: Routledge, 2000.

*Galen: On the Natural Faculties.* Translated by A. J. Brock. Loeb Classical Library. Cambridge: Harvard University Press, 1916.

Gellius, Aulus. *Attic Nights*. Bks. I–XX. Translated by J. C. Rolfe. Loeb Classical Library. Cambridge: Harvard University Press, 1927.

Gerard, John. *The Herball or General Historie of plantes. Gathered by John Gerard of London, master in Chirurgerie*. London: 1597.

*Good Hous-wives Treasurie, The*. London: Edward Allde, 1588.

*Goodman of Paris, The (Le menagier de Paris): a treatise on moral and domestic economy by a citizen of Paris* (c. 1393). Translated with an introduction and notes by Eileen Power. London: G. Routledge and Sons, 1928.

Hester, Harriet H. *300 Sugar Saving Recipes*. New York: M. Barrows and Co., 1942.

Hill, A. P. *House-keeping Made Easy*. New York: J. O. Kane, 1867.

Hines, Duncan. *Adventures in Good Cooking*. Bowling Green, Ky.: Adventures in Good Eating, Inc., 1939.

*Indian Cook Book, The*. Indian Women's Club of Tulsa. Tulsa, Okla.: Self-published, 1933.

Leslie, Eliza. *Directions for cookery; being a system of the art, in its various branches*. Philadelphia: E. L. Carey and A. Hart, 1837.

Lincoln, Mary J. *Mrs. Lincoln's Boston Cook Book*. Boston: Roberts Brothers, 1883.

Longe, Sarah. *Receipt Book*. Folger Shakespeare Library Collection, Washington, D.C.

*Manual for Army Cooks*. Washington, D.C.: U.S. Government Printing Office, 1910.

Markham, Gervase. *The English Housewife*. London: Printed by John Wolfe for Edward White, 1587.

May, Robert. *The Accomplish't Cook*. London: Printed for O. Blagrave, 1685.

Murrell, John. *Murrells Two Books of Cookerie and Carving*. London: Printed by M.F. for John Marriot, 1631. And London: 1638.

*New Mexico Cookery*. Santa Fe: State Land Office, 1916.

Partridge, John. *The good Huswifes Handmaide for the Kitchin*. Imprinted by Richard Jones, 1594.

Plat, Sir Hugh. *Delightes for Ladies*. London: Printed by P. Short, 1603.

Platina. *On Right Pleasure and Good Health*. A critical edition and translation by Mary Ella Milham. Tempe, Ariz.: Medieval and Renaissance Text and Studies, 1998.

Randolph, Mary. *The Virginia House-wife*. Washington: Davis and Force, 1824.

Rees, Nigel. *Cassell's Movie Quotations*. London: Cassell and Co., 2000.

Rombauer, Irma S. *The Joy of Cooking*. St. Louis: A. C. Clayton Printing Co., 1931.

Rorer, Mrs. S. T. *Mrs. Rorer's Philadelphia Cook Book*. Philadelphia: Arnold and Co., 1886.

Ruscelli, Girolamo. *The Secretes of the Reverende Maister Alexis of Piemovnt.* Translated from French to English by Wyllyam Warde. London: Printed by John Kingstone for Nicolas Inglande, 1558.

Scappi, Bartolomeo. *Opera di Bartolomeo Scappi M. dell'Arte del Cucinare.* Venice: Presso Alessandro Vecchi, 1610.

Scott, Michael. *The Philosopher's Banquet . . . The second Edition newly corrected and enlarged, to almost as much more. By W. B. Esquire.* London: Printed by T.C. for Leonard Becket, 1614.

*Select Papyri, Non-Literary Papyri, Private Affairs.* Translated by A. S. Hunt and C. C. Edgar. Loeb Classical Library. Cambridge: Harvard University Press, 1932.

Simmons, Amelia. *American Cookery, or the art of dressing viands, fish, poultry and vegetables.* Hartford: Hudson and Goodwin, 1796.

*Texas Cook Book.* Edited by the Ladies' Association of the First Presbyterian Church. Houston: Self-published, 1883.

Ulmer, Mary, and Beck, Samuel, eds. *Cherokee Cooklore.* Cherokee, N.C.: Museum of the Cherokee Indian, 1951.

*Viandier of Taillevent, The.* Edited and translated by Terence Scully. Ottawa: University of Ottawa Press, 1988.

Webb, Margaret J., ed. *Early English Recipes, Selected from the Harleian Ms. 279 of About 1430 A.D.* Cambridge: Harvard University Press, 1937.

Webb, Nancy. *Parties for Pennies.* New York: M. Barrows and Co., 1942.

Winn-Smith, Alice B. *Thrifty Cooking for Wartime.* New York: Macmillan Co., 1942.

## INTERNET RESOURCES

The Internet Movie Database: www.imdb.com

# INDEX

## About the Author

FRANCINE SEGAN is a psychologist and food historian. She lectures at museums, historic homes, schools, and theaters and consults on historic menu planning. Segan and her husband, Marc, an inventor and theater producer, along with their two children, Samantha and Max, divide their time between New York City, the Berkshires, and Italy.